KT-226-616

SH✳T HAPPENS

The Book

BY DEBBIE LAZARUS

WORKMAN PUBLISHING, NEW YORK

Copyright © 2006 by Debbie Lazarus

All rights reserved. No portion of this book may be reproduced—
mechanically, electronically, or by any other means, including
photocopying—without written permission of the publisher.
Published simultaneously in Canada by Thomas Allen & Son
Limited.

Library of Congress Cataloging-in-Publication Data is available

ISBN-10: 0-7611-4436-6
ISBN-13: 978-0-7611-4436-6

Workman books are available at special discount when purchased
in bulk for premiums and sales promotions as well as for fund-
raising or educational use. Special editions or book excerpts also
can be created to specification. For details, contact the Special
Sales Director at the address below.

Cover Design by Paul Hanson
Interior Design by Paul Hanson and Patrick Borelli

Workman Publishing Company, Inc.
225 Varick Street
New York, NY 10014-4381

www.workman.com

Printed in the United States of America

First Printing November 2006

10 9 8 7 6 5 4 3 2

SH✳T HAPPENS

The Book

To my Mom and Dad

———

Acknowledgments

At Workman Publishing: Thanks to Leora Kahn, for over 20 years of friendship and fun. This book wouldn't exist without you. Thanks to Cassie Murdoch, Richard Rosen, and James Wehrle, for all their sage advice and unflagging support. Special thanks to Jennifer Griffin, who shepherded this project through its many incarnations with great humor, insight, and faith in its ultimate success.

And warmest thanks to my family—my children, Eve and Simon, who put up with cold dinners and competition for workspace at the kichen table while I raced to meet my deadlines, and my husband, Rob, who's always been there when sh*t's happened to me.

Introduction

From his earliest beginnings, man has asked himself, Why does sh*t happen? All we know is that sometimes we are the innocent victims of Providence and sometimes we create our own trouble—by giving in to folly and stupidity, by refusing to learn from the past, or by cohabiting with wild animals we've mistaken for pets.

We're not talking about you, of course. You listen to meteorologists, refrain from setting hornets' nests on fire, and never get hit by falling seagulls. This book is about those other people. The ones to whom sh*t always seems to happen. As you read these accounts of unhappy happenings, take comfort in the fact that somewhere, someone is having a much worse day than you.

LIFE IS A BANQUET: EAT UP

When life seems like an all-you-can-eat buffet, it's hard to turn down the offering, even if you'll have to answer to the authorities or wind up with a fatal case of indigestion.

SMORGASBORD IS THE LAW OF THE JUNGLE

1999: Responding to the encroachment of housing development in Rio de Janeiro on the surrounding jungle, a ravenous, seven-foot-long alligator decided to treat a nearby suburban backyard as its personal snack bar. It helped itself to a pet dog and four chickens. Police arrived as it was finishing its meal and, after a 30-minute scuffle, escorted it to a local zoo.

DANGER
KEEP OUT
ALLIGATORS

BAMBI PULLS INSIDE JOB ON BIG SNAKE

Summer 2002: A 14-foot python in northern India figured he'd made the catch of a lifetime when he eagerly swallowed a 90-pound chital deer. Unfortunately for him, what he'd caught was a fatal case of indigestion. While local villagers feasted their eyes on his super-gorged stomach, the python could do little but lie immobilized on the forest floor. He died five days later, and when veterinarians opened him up they found the deer's body still intact inside his gut.

CANNIBAL EATS AWAY POLITICAL ADVANTAGE

1873-1874: Instead of leading the five men who'd hired him through the San Juan Mountains in Colorado, Alfred Packer decided to sit out the winter in the mountains, feasting on his charges. Packer showed up in town the next spring, fat and fit and flashing a wad of bills. A local Indian chief who'd stumbled on Packer's devilish camp exposed his crimes, but Packer escaped. He didn't stand trial until ten years later, when he became the only cannibal ever convicted in the United States court system. He was sentenced to die but managed to elude the hangman's noose and was finally paroled in 1901.

At the sentencing, the judge had given one possible motive for Packer's crime: "There was only six Democrats in all of Hinsdale County and you ate five of them."

ILLEGAL IMMIGRANTS WHET BIG CATS' APPETITES

1998: While leading a night viewing expedition through Kruger National Park in South Africa, a field guide was killed and eaten by a leopard before the horrified eyes of the tourists. He was the eighth human to be attacked and eaten in the park within two years, and park rangers feared he would not be the last. It seems that illegal immigrants seeking work had been using the park as a thoroughfare. The lions, leopards, and other large cats quickly realized that pedestrians make an easy snack, and they lost any hesitation to attack unsuspecting passersby.

INUIT INADVERTENTLY
EATS
SCIENCE PROJECT

2002: Puzzled scientists wondered what had happened to a goose that had gone missing from their migratory tracking project. The goose was one of six that had been fitted with a satellite transmitter, which beamed its progress from Northern Ireland to the Canadian Arctic. When the goose suddenly moved from one Arctic island to another and then stopped completely, the scientists grew suspicious and asked local authorities to find it. The Canadians finally located it—in an Inuit's freezer. The hunter, unaware of the goose's affiliation, had shot it and taken it home for dinner.

OOOOPS!

Builders bulldoze the wrong house, runaway trains barrel through stations, wayward dinnerware causes a car accident, and other man-made and natural blunders

WRECKING BALL HITS WRONG HOUSE

2003: A homeowner in Phoenix, Arizona, would have hit the ceiling—if she'd still had one—when she arrived home to find her house had been demolished by mistake. House numbers on the block weren't clearly marked, and the demolition crew, which had been hired to raze the vacant, boarded-up house across the street, got confused.

THE ROCK THAT ALMOST
FLATTENED
PITTSBURGH

June 1938: Citizens of Pittsburgh, Pennsylvania, were surprised to see a bright, fast-moving light in the sky overhead. It was a 500-ton meteor that had passed through Earth's atmosphere and was burning up as it sped toward the ground. It landed just outside the city with a terrific bang. Scientists who examined the rock and its crater said it would have destroyed much of the city if it had landed there.

THE "FEDERAL EXPRESS" PLOWS INTO UNION STATION

January 15, 1953:
Unable to stop because of faulty brakes, the *Federal Express* railway train  plowed right through Union Station in Washington, D.C., tearing through the concourse, shops, newspaper stands, and stationmaster's office, until it finally came to rest in the waiting room. A minute later the floor gave way, sending the locomotive and two cars into the baggage room below. Miraculously, no one was killed because the train, which was carrying guests to President Eisenhower's inauguration, blasted its whistle and cleared the station as it came rushing through.

COASTER LEAVES PASSENGERS HANGING

2003: A roller coaster at an amusement park in Maryland came to a sudden stop due to a computer or hydraulics glitch, leaving a car of more than 20 people dangling upside down high above the park. Rescue workers waited nearby with ladders but decided it was safer to wait and see if park maintenance workers could get the ride started again. They eventually did—bringing the passengers down from the 100-foot height more than two hours after their ordeal began.

JAPANESE TURN SIMULATION INTO REAL LANDSLIDE

November 11, 1971: In an effort to learn more about landslides, scientists at Japan's Agency of Science and Technology created an artificial one by soaking a 60-foot hill outside Kawasaki with water to simulate a torrential downpour. The simulation was so accurate that the hillside gave way, engulfing the scientists in a nine-foot-deep sea of mud and rocks. Fifteen of them were killed while TV journalists captured the whole incident on tape.

BROKEN
GLACIER MAKES
BIGGEST SPLASH
OF ALL

July 9, 1958: The biggest wave in recorded history was not a tsunami. It was a giant splash wave created by a slab of rock and ice (300 million cubic meters' worth) that broke off the face of the Lituya Glacier, north of Juneau, Alaska, after an earthquake. It created a wave approximately 1,750 feet high that washed over a mountain on the opposite shore of Lituya Bay. Many boats in the harbor were swallowed by the wave, but one lucky boat, the *Badger,* was lifted so high that it was deposited intact into the ocean on the far side of the inlet.

PLEASE KNOCK BEFORE ENTERING . . .

2002: A Hollywood, Florida, couple was interrupted during dinner by a bulldozer that plowed into the back of their home and began demolishing it. They ran outside and managed to stop the operator from tearing off the entire roof. He had gotten the address of his demolition job wrong, and the contracting company doing teardowns in the area promised to pay for the damages.

Trouble ahead: With the typical optimism of an experienced contractor, the owner of the company said, "I can fix it in two days."

KEEPING THE HOME FIRES BURNING

1962: In Centralia, Pennsylvania, trash burning in an open pit lit an exposed vein of coal underground. The fire spread through an extensive network of coal mines and veins and has been burning ever since. In 1985, Centralia was declared "municipalia non gratis" by the federal government, which gave its citizens money to relocate; Centralia now is practically a ghost town. The fire could last until all the underground coal in the region burns itself out.

You ain't seen nothin' yet: A fire in a coalfield in Northwest China has been burning for more than 100 years.

RAILROAD BARRELS TO ICONIC STATUS

October 22, 1895: A train that was traveling from Granville into the Montparnasse Station in Paris overran its buffer stop, crossed the station concourse, crashed through a two-foot-thick wall, and fell 30 feet onto the Place de Rennes.

Miraculously, only one person, a street vendor, was killed. A photo of the train spilling out of the station onto the street has been a bestseller ever since.

CUP OF COFFEE
KILLS
SUBURBANITE

1949: Wanting to savor one last cup, a Westchester housewife brought her coffee along on the ride to the station where her husband started his morning commute. She placed the cup on the seat next to her, and when it began to tip over, her husband, who was at the wheel, reached across to stop it. He lost control of the car, plunging it over an embankment and into a stone wall. The wife was killed and the husband was badly hurt. The coffee cup survived the wreckage unscathed.

TITANIC *TROUBLE*

- Shortly before midnight on April 14, 1912, the R.M.S. *Titanic* struck an iceberg off the banks of Newfoundland and sank in less than three hours. Delay in evacuating the ship, lack of radio contact with nearby vessels, and having only enough lifeboats for half the passengers and crew contributed to the appalling death toll, which exceeded 1,500.

- In 1916, while serving as a hospital ship in the Aegean Sea during World War I, the White Star Liner *Brittanic* (the *Titanic*'s sister ship) struck a submerged mine and sank, killing 52 people on board.

- Although there have been many successful *Titanic*-themed films, including the James Cameron record-breaking 1997 blockbuster, producer Lew Grade's bomb, *Raise the Titanic*, only gave him that sinking feeling. His comment on losing more than $40 million in production money: "It would have been cheaper to lower the Atlantic."

- Since its discovery at the bottom of the North Atlantic in 1985, so many people have visited the wreck of the *Titanic*— including a couple who were married in a submersible on its bow— that the ship is now rotting away at an accelerated rate. It is estimated that the famous wreck will disintegrate within 150 years.

ART ATTACK

Art is supposed to

inspire awesome

feelings in us.

Unfortunately,

sometimes they get a

little too awesome . . .

LOCALS GRILL CHEESE ARTIST

2001: Civic leaders in tiny Powell, Wyoming, thought it would be both interesting and profitable to allow a visiting New York artist to spray-coat a vacant house inside and out with cheese. Neighbors of the "Wyoming Cheese House" were less sanguine. They were convinced not only that the project would attract assorted varmints (birds, rats, and curiosity seekers) to the normally quiet neighborhood, but also that before the house was demolished—or consumed—it would stink up the area. As for the artist, he felt the house would be a celebration of living: "It's milk. It's life."

MODERN BALLET MOVES AUDIENCE TO JEERS

May 29, 1913: Innovative art is not always favorably reviewed, but the premiere performance of Igor Stravinsky's ballet *The Rite of Spring* so agitated its conservative Parisian audience that rioting nearly broke out in the theater. Stravinsky's discordant music, coupled with the sensuous dancing of the Russian ballet star Vaslav Nijinsky, caused some members of the audience to loudly complain. When other audience members tried to shut them up, fistfights broke out

in the aisles. Police ejected the most belligerent offenders, but fighting continued until the end of the performance. The show's producers considered it a great success.

The Da Vinci Curse

- **1495:** Seeking a more flexible medium than traditional fresco (which had been successfully used for centuries), Leonardo da Vinci used a new technique (an oil-and-tempera paint applied over a base coat of gesso, pitch, and mastic) for his mural, *The Last Supper.* It seemed like a good idea at the time, but within a few years of its completion, the painting began to flake off the wall.

- **1482-1499:** After Leonardo spent 16 years designing and executing a life-size terra-cotta model for an equestrian monument to Francesco Sforza, Duke of Milan, Sforza fell from power and the bronze casting of the colossal statue was doomed. Invading French troops later destroyed the model by using it for target practice.

- **1500-1508:** Undaunted by his failed experiments in *The Last Supper*, Leonardo cooked up a new paint concoction for his monumental painting of the Battle of Anghiari. After the paint ran, he abandoned the project, which survives only in drawings by other artists.

- **1519:** Leonardo died in France and was buried in the church of Saint-Florentin in the Château d'Amboise. During the reign of Napoleon, the church—including all its graves—was desecrated and destroyed. Sixty years later, during an excavation of the Saint-Florentin, a skeleton believed to be Leonardo's was moved to its final resting place in the nearby chapel of Saint-Hubert.

- **2002:** A recently rediscovered Leonardo da Vinci drawing of Orpheus and the Furies slipped back into obscurity thanks to the efforts of the restorers who were trying to clean it. Without first testing the ink and paper, restorers submerged the drawing in a standard solution of alcohol and distilled water, which immediately dissolved the delicate vegetable dyes Leonardo used.

SOMETIMES THE SKY
REALLY IS FALLING . . .

IT'S RAINING—WINDOWS!

January 20, 1973: The Hancock Tower in Boston had an innovative design that covered a traditional steel frame entirely with glass. During its construction a particularly nasty windstorm blew out several dozen of the floor-to-ceiling panels, which crashed back into the building's façade, shattering more glass, before finally hurtling to the streets below. Luckily no one was hurt. Wooden patches were placed on a third of the building before engineers realized that the entire façade, more than 10,000 double-glass panels, had to be replaced with tempered single-pane glass.

CASTING FATE TO THE WINDS

Next time you're

tempted to toss

something out the

window, remember

what happened to these

unlucky folks.

SHORTS RESULT IN
WIDESPREAD
SHORTS

2002: At the height of a domestic disturbance
between a couple in Augsburg,
Germany, the boyfriend flung
his lederhosen out the
window. They landed on
the electric lines of the
city's tram system, shorted
out the circuitry, shut down
the trams, and caused
massive gridlock on
all the local roads.
The man had to
pay to have the
lederhosen
removed and
the damage
repaired.

THE WINDSOR HOTEL
FIRE

March 17, 1899: While watching the St. Patrick's Day Parade passing below on Fifth Avenue, a guest at the renowned Windsor Hotel absentmindedly threw a lighted match out the window. It ignited a curtain and flames spread quickly. The hotel staff was on it immediately, but the fire alarm box was located across the street (and through the parade route). When one of the staff attempted to cross to the call box, he was rebuffed several times by a policeman, who did not believe him until the crowd around him screamed, "Look! The Windsor's on fire!" The delay ensured that the hotel was completely destroyed.

LAZY CHRISTMAS CLEANUP CAUSES BLACKOUT

December 1999: Faced with hauling his used Christmas tree to the sidewalk, one Pittsburgh man decided it would be faster and more efficient to simply fling it out the window. On its way down, the tree hit some electrical lines and knocked out power to more than 400 homes and businesses. The man's unfortunate neighbors spent half their day in the dark, and although the act was not technically illegal, police considered pressing charges against him.

SOMETIMES THE SKY
REALLY IS FALLING . . .

IT'S RAINING—FISH!

February 1974: During a tropical storm, 150-plus silver perch rained down on a sheep farm in Australia. Fish often fall from the sky. It is believed that waterspouts over the ocean suck them up along with great quantities of water, which they then dump on land during storms and hurricanes.

FOR THE BIRDS

Their ancestors ruled

the world during the

Jurassic period, and

these feisty avians

won't let us forget it.

KAMIKAZE CROWS
TERRORIZE
TOKYO

2001: Thousands of aggressive crows attacked pedestrians in Tokyo and its suburbs. The birds had a special penchant for cyclists, many of whom fell off their bicycles and injured themselves while trying to avoid the incoming crows.

A burgeoning crow population, which had swelled to more than 30,000, was responsible for the problem. Animal-control experts raided crows' nests, removing eggs and hatchlings, to reduce the population.

BUZZARD
BAGS BOEING

2003: In what must have looked like a message from hell itself, a vulture collided with a Boeing 737 that had just taken off from an airport in Brazil. The bird smashed into the cockpit window and broke it, forcing the pilot to make an emergency landing. Everyone on the plane was safe. The vulture, needless to say, was never the same again.

WILD TURKEYS
TRY TO COME IN FROM THE COLD

2002: Like Depression-era hobos knocking on doors and asking for a handout, wild turkeys invaded a Chicago suburb, banging on doors and windows, trying to get residents to come out and feed them. Officials believed they were game birds that had been illegally released into a local state park. Police managed to capture one turkey that had been living the good life in the backyard of a local resident, but feared the others would eventually become supper for coyotes.

POLLY WANTS A PRIME MINISTER

April 3, 1998: During an environmental summit in England at which the problems of disappearing wildlife were addressed, a rare red-headed macaw attacked deputy prime minister John Prescott during a photo shoot. The large parrot bit Prescott's finger and wouldn't let go. The bird's keeper was finally able to pull him off. Prescott's only comment on his painful encounter with the ungrateful bird: "That's wildlife for you."

HORNY TURKEY SEEKS LIKE-MINDED FOWL AT VIDEO STORE

2002: One night during mating season, a 12-pound tom turkey crashed through the front window of a video store and proceeded to trash the place, scattering videos and cases, knocking down displays, and clearly expressing his disdain for the hunting videos by relieving himself on them. Animal experts speculated that the tom was drawn to the hunting section by pictures of avian beauties on the boxes. Like many a Romeo wannabe, he retreated from his carnal frustrations to the science-fiction section, where police found him the next morning.

MOOR HOOTER
BANNED
IN BRITAIN

2002: A huge Eurasian eagle owl, known in Britain as the "Beast of Ilkley Moor," was captured after two years of hell-raising. The owl either had been illegally released by its owner or had escaped from a collection of exotic animals. The nonnative predator was known to feast on indigenous birds and swoop down on area residents, but the last straw came with its attack on a small child.

RILED RESIDENTS SQUAWK ABOUT FOWL LANGUAGE

2000: Residents of a South Pasadena apartment complex turned to city hall to solve their two-year dispute with a neighbor who owned a rude parrot. They claimed the ill-mannered bird sat outside all day whistling, screaming, cursing, and harassing them as they swam in the pool below its terrace—and that the parrot's owner refused to keep it inside. The owner countered that the bird needed fresh air for its health and that it had picked up its salty language from the disgruntled neighbors.

@#!!

THE ROAD TO HELL

This is a puzzling world, and Old Harry's* got a finger in it.

—GEORGE ELIOT

*the Devil

ROUTE 666

AROUSES DRIVERS' FEARS

May 2002: A rural two-lane highway in Alberta, Canada, was the scene of two auto fatalities in three weeks, prompting some local residents to wonder if Highway 666 is cursed. Four fender-benders and another nonfatal accident took place in the preceding year. Local officials don't think the number is causing the accidents and likened it to the 13th floor in many buildings. A friend of one of the men killed on the road also thinks it wasn't Satan's work, but rather the lack of speed limits on tight bends in the highway.

DEVIL WORSHIPPER PROPELS SELF TO NEXT DIMENSION

June 17, 1952: John Whiteside Parsons, a pioneering rocket engineer at Caltech and a founding member of the Jet Propulsion Laboratory, propelled himself to kingdom come one night in his Los Angeles mansion. The mansion had been the site of many black magic rituals, including drug-induced sex orgies hosted by Parsons, who was an ardent follower of notorious occultist Aleister Crowley. Many believed Parsons was following a recipe from one of Crowley's sacred texts to conjure a homunculus—an otherworldly being whose magic powers would be at Parsons's disposal—when the experiment blew up in his face.

DEVILISH TATTOO OPENS DOOR TO HELLISH VIRUS

2003: A California man who contracted a flesh-eating virus blamed it on the tattoo parlor he had visited to cover a tattoo on his neck that upset his coworkers. Workers at the parlor said their tools were sterile and the man, who neglected to keep the new tattoo covered, could have contracted the virus anywhere. Perhaps it was his tattoo that was to blame: It included the f-word and the number "666."

A TRIP TO THE UNDERWORLD

Much less fun than Alice had—unfortunate occurrences remind us we aren't really living on the ground floor.

EARTHQUAKE

GIVES ITALIANS SHORT GLIMPSE OF

UNDERWORLD

February 5, 1783: A series of five earthquakes rocked Calabria, Italy, destroying towns and killing thousands. Thermal springs erupted underground, causing 100-foot-wide fissures to open on the surface that swallowed up people and animals—who were soon shot back to Earth by boiling geysers. Although they were badly burned, many survived their trip to hell.

SINKHOLE MAKES GIANT NOISE IN FOREST THOUGH NO ONE IS THERE TO HEAR IT

December 2, 1972: A resident of Shelby County, Alabama, felt his house shaking and heard trees breaking and a loud roaring noise outside. Nothing seemed to be amiss in the immediate area, but two days later hunters discovered a sinkhole in the woods measuring 425 feet long, 350 feet wide, and 150 feet deep. Dubbed the "December Giant," it is the largest sinkhole ever reported in the United States.

TWIN SINKHOLES
EAT CAR,
EYE EATERY

2002: Heavy rains in Hickory, North Carolina, opened up two 50-foot-wide sinkholes in the parking lot of Buffalo's Southwest Café. One hole, more than 100 feet deep, swallowed a Corvette. City officials quickly declared the kitchen closed.

After almost a year of battling city officials, who wanted the property condemned, the café reopened in June 2003. In addition to the regular menu, it now sold postcards and T-shirts that read "We're a hole lotta fun."

HOME IS WHERE THE HELL IS

A man's home

may be his castle,

but that doesn't

mean he's in charge.

HUSBAND CLEANS OUT GARAGE, SELLS FAMILY'S PAST

Summer 2002: When his wife took their kids for a two-week visit to her parents, an overeager Tulsa, Oklahoma, man held a garage sale that netted him over $1,000 and a cleaned-out garage. When his wife returned she discovered he had sold her priceless mementos, including infant clothes, a doll collection, and a framed map handed down from her grandfather. To try and buy back their treasures, the couple appeared on local radio and TV news, offering to pay $3 for every $1 spent. They also took out a newspaper ad headlined "Husband in the Doghouse." The woman got back the map and her dolls, but no one returned the baby clothes—which she had wanted most of all.

KITCHEN GOES TO THE DOGS; DOG GOES TO THE CELLAR

2001: A big, hungry dog whose family was still at church couldn't wait for Sunday dinner and decided to fix himself a little something. While rummaging around on the counters, he knocked a big bag of dog food onto the stove, which he also managed to turn on. When his family got home they discovered their house filled with smoke, the kitchen a charred wreck, and the culprit hiding in the basement, presumably still hungry.

CUTTHROAT COT GRABS GERMAN

2003: A German man was removing a blanket from a drawer inside a folding bed when the contraption suddenly snapped shut. He was trapped until, hours later, neighbors finally heard his screams and called police, who said the man was so tightly jammed inside that he would never have been able to free himself.

PARROT PARROTS WAILING WOMAN

2003: Police in Tucson, Arizona, were sent to a house after a 911 hang-up call. When they heard a damsel in distress screaming inside, they called firefighters to bring a battering ram to break down the door. Once inside, the rescuers found that the woman they thought they were rescuing was nothing but a big male parrot whooping it up in its cage.

SNAKE'S SITZ BATH ENDS IN CATASTROPHE

1998: Instead of accompanying its owner to a Super Bowl party, a 95-pound, 12-foot python stayed home for its routine soak in the tub. When it slithered out to dry off, it brushed against the faucet and turned it on, flooding the apartment and the one below. Police charged the owner, who had been the subject of previous complaints, with harboring a dangerous animal.

Denial is bliss: In his defense, the owner said, "A lot of people have dogs or cats that get out of hand, but no one ever hears of snakes biting or hurting anyone."

DYIN' IN THE BATHTUB . . .

You'd think a warm, relaxing bath is the one place you could safely get away from it all. However, history proves it's the ultimate place to get "caught with your pants down":

- **A.D. 192:** Considered an utter disgrace for competing as a gladiator in the Colosseum, the Roman Emperor Commodus suffered the indignity of being strangled in his own bath.

- **1793:** French Revolutionary newspaper publisher and psoriasis sufferer Jean-Paul Marat was known to spend the whole day in the bath to mollify his painful skin condition. His political enemies, convinced his strident cries for blood needed to be silenced, sent Charlotte Corday there to stab him to death one afternoon.

- **1971:** Hard-living, hard-drinking Doors lead singer Jim Morrison was found dead in the tub in his Paris hotel room. Although many believe he died of a typical out-of-control–rock-star drug overdose or by choking on his own vomit, the coroner ruled it a heart attack. No autopsy was ever performed.

- **1978:** French singer Claude François got the life shocked out of him when he changed a light bulb while standing in a tubful of bathwater.

60

ROAD SPILLS

The heavenly, the

smelly, the annoying,

the buzzing, and

the sticky—things

that literally

"fell off a truck."

ALABAMA OFFICIALS SOUR ON SWEET SYRUP

2001: Cullman, Alabama, officials found themselves in a sticky situation when a huge rig overturned on a steep grade near the Vest Creek Bridge, dumping almost 5,000 gallons of molasses onto the roadway. The molasses oozed over the bridge and into the creek, prompting environmental crews to take immediate measures to stop the syrupy substance from polluting local rivers and lakes. On land, a three-inch layer of slippery goo covered the highway, which had to be shut down for over ten hours while crews armed with sawdust and scrapers scooped up the mess.

PUNY PORKERS PERPETRATE PARKWAY PARALYSIS

2003: A truck carrying baby pigs overturned on Interstate 40 in Oklahoma, spilling all 800 into the road. The highway was shut down in both directions while rescue personnel tracked down the scurrying little piggies before they could invade nearby suburbs.

TRUCK MISHAP HAS WHOLE TOWN BUZZING

1998: A tractor-trailer transporting hives from a honey farm in southeastern Wisconsin caught its back tires in a ditch and overturned in an intersection in Germantown. No one was hurt, but many of the four to five million bees in the truck escaped. The road was closed for more than eight hours while police cleared the area.

FUNERAL BECOMES STREET THEATER

2002: A car carrying a coffin to a funeral in Chile was rammed by a truck and the casket and flowers were thrown onto the road. The grieving relatives tried for more than an hour to hail a cab, but no one stopped to help them—passersby thought it was performance art staged in honor of Chilean surrealist painter Roberto Matta Echaurren, who had died the same day.

JOHNNY HITS THE ROAD

2003: Drivers on Interstate 5 in Washington feared the worst when a truck carrying Portosans jackknifed, tossing portable toilets onto the road. Luckily the johns were heading to a new job and were filled only with blue sanitation liquid.

DRIVERS CRY OVER SPILLED MILK

2002: While driving south on a California interstate, the driver of a tanker truck fell asleep. His rig drifted across the southbound lanes, hit two cars and the center divider, then overturned. The accident caused an unusual flood—5,000 gallons of milk that required hours of cleanup—but only minor injuries to the truck driver.

"DREAM COME TRUE" CAUSES

NIGHTMARE

2003: In what one policeman described as the "best accident ever," a tanker truck overturned on a highway in São Paolo, Brazil, spilling liquid chocolate across the entire three-lane road. Children flocked to the scene to gulp down the ambrosia—some stripped and rolled around in it. It was not so sweet for drivers in the seven-mile traffic jam, who had to wait hours for the road to be cleared.

SOMETIMES THE SKY REALLY IS FALLING . . .

IT'S RAINING— SEAGULLS!

Residents of British Columbia were surprised when a flock of dead seagulls suddenly plummeted from the sky. The scavenger birds had been gorging on tossed-out Valentine's Day chocolate at a local garbage dump. The caffeine and theobromine, two ingredients in chocolate that are toxic to many animals, did them in.

LOOK, IT SAYS "GULLIBLE" ON THE CEILING . . .

It turns out you can

fool a lot of people

a lot of the time.

BBC BROADCAST CAUSES
PANIC

1926: Despite the BBC's announcement that the program was fictional, London-area residents were riled by a radio drama that described rioting in the city, the burning of the Houses of Parliament and Big Ben, and the hanging of ministers by an angry mob. Hundreds of hysterical listeners called police, newspapers, and the BBC. People jammed roads trying to escape or to get into the city to rescue their friends and relatives. The BBC finally suspended the show in the middle and apologized the next day.

PAPER HAWKS HOAX TO BIRD-BRAINED PUBLIC

1927: Chicago-area newspapers received an unexpected circulation bonanza when the *Chicago Journal* printed a story about the sighting of a huge hawk near the Art Institute. After the story ran on the newspaper's front page, reports of other hawk sightings poured in to the *Journal* and other Chicago dailies. Some citizens took to patrolling the streets with guns to fend off the hawks. Finally, when editors at the *Journal* revealed that the original report was part of a fiction serial, the hysteria ended almost overnight, but not before even more papers explaining what had happened were sold.

WORLD WAR ZERO STARTS IN NEW JERSEY

October 30, 1938: When Orson Welles adapted H. G. Wells's *War of the Worlds* for a special Halloween eve radio performance, he wanted to make it topical and realistic by changing its setting to Grover's Mill, New Jersey, and presenting it as a series of news broadcasts. Welles succeeded beyond his wildest dreams: Listeners, especially those who tuned in late and missed the introductory disclaimers, thought they were hearing a real invasion from outer space. Residents of New Jersey began patrolling the countryside with guns, looking for Martians. Others panicked, called police, or took to their cars to escape. Welles apologized the next day, though he could hardly be faulted—the program included several announcements that it was a presentation of the Mercury Theater of the Air, but apparently people were too agitated to take them seriously.

CRACKS IN COLOSSEUM CAUSE CHAOS

May 18, 1954: Huge cracks appeared in Rome's Colosseum, a building that had endured centuries of pillage, earthquakes, and neglect, yet remained structurally intact. Thanks to an old proverb—"Rome and the world are safe, so long as the Colosseum stands"—thousands panicked on learning of the cracks. On Monday, May 24, the day a local doomsayer predicted would be the day of Rome's destruction, citizens poured into Vatican City, seeking absolution for their sins and praying that God would spare the world. Annoyed Vatican officials assured the crowds that "the world will see Tuesday and more Tuesdays to come."

ALIENS ORDER BRITISH TO DISARM

November 26, 1977:
Viewers of the nightly newscast on England's Southern Television had a close encounter of the third kind when a disembodied voice interrupted the broadcast and warned them to

destroy "all your weapons of evil." The alien peacemaker identified himself as Glon of the Asteron Galactic Command. In reality, he was a hoaxer who had patched into the TV station's transmitter. True to most such hoaxes, hundreds of listeners panicked and called the station and police.

LOOKING FOR LOVE IN ALL THE WRONG PLACES

For these unfortunates,

love is blind—especially

to the consequences of

their out-of-control lust.

CHARLIE CHAPLIN IN THE HOT SEAT, PART 1

January 1927: When Charlie Chaplin, 35, married his 16-year-old pregnant girlfriend, Lita Grey, the tabloids had a field day. But it was nothing compared to the publicity generated by their bitter divorce three years later, during which Lita accused him of forcing her to commit "perverse acts" and threatened to name his famous partners in adultery. To protect his friends, Chaplin acquiesced to Grey's ransom-size settlement of $825,000, leaving him free to move on to his next "Lolita."

The silver lining for Charlie: Lita's money-grubbing relatives, who had been living with the couple, finally moved out.

SUMMER FUN IN THE SUN

Sometimes you just want to have a little fun, but the law gets in your way:

- In July 2005, coast guard boats rushed to answer screams coming from a boat in the waters off the coast of Devon, England, only to find a couple noisily making love.

- Later that same summer, a Dutch couple, too impassioned to wait until they got home, were arrested for having sex on top of a police car. They failed to notice that two officers were seated inside the car.

- And in February 2006, an Argentinean woman fulfilled her fantasy of having sex in broad daylight outside the local mayor's office before she and her partner were arrested.

WOMAN UNHARMED, MAN UN-ARMED

2002: Late one night, two men in Marion County, Indiana, offered a ride to an exotic dancer in exchange for sexual favors. When she feared they weren't going to take her home, she attacked the driver. He lost control of the car and struck a telephone pole, ripping off his friend's arm, which had been sticking out the car window. The dancer eventually got home safely, but the injured man's hand was never found.

ROBOT WORKER EXHIBITS TYPICAL MAIL BEHAVIOR

1998: In a scene reminiscent of predatory coworkers everywhere, a 500-pound robot used to deliver mail got over his inhibitions and pinned an attractive female employee against a file cabinet. The woman had been reaching for her batch of mail when the lusty robot attacked. She hit his stop button, but he continued to put the moves on her. The woman  filed suit against her company, claiming injuries to her shoulder, back, and legs. The company countered that, because the droid moved at a snail's pace, it was hard to imagine that his unwanted advances could trap her.

CHARLIE CHAPLIN IN THE HOT SEAT, PART 2

1943: Chaplin found himself in trouble again when a former protégée, Joan Barry, sued him for support, claiming he was the father of her unborn child. Reporters packing the courtroom heard the usual tales of sordid seduction, which were duly blared in the headlines the next day. Despite blood tests proving he was not the child's father (which were not admissible in court), the jury still found him liable and ordered him to pay. The 54-year-old Chaplin soon left the country with his new bride, 18-year-old Oona O'Neill.

SHY SNAKE BITES ARDENT SUITOR

2003: Like a teenage boy showing off his new girlfriend to his buddies, the owner of a two-foot rattlesnake wrapped the serpent around his own neck and started kissing it in front of his disconcerted friends, whose worst fears were realized when the snake bit the man on the lips after a couple of kisses. The suitor survived, but his slithery paramour met its maker under one friend's boot.

GO(AT)IN' TO THE CHAPEL OF LOVE

2006: After a man in Sudan was caught in a compromising position with a goat, the local council elders, instead of turning him in to the police, forced him to pay a proper bride's price to the goat's owner. After the dowry exchanged hands, the goat-bride went home with her new husband!

ANIMAL HOUSE

When a couple of

dogs and cats just

aren't enough

DENIZEN OF EDEN TURNS GARDEN PEST

2003: A New York City man who wanted to create a "Garden of Eden" in his Harlem housing project faced reckless endangerment charges for keeping a 400-pound tiger and a five-foot-long alligator in his fifth-floor apartment. Authorities became aware of the situation when the man sought treatment at a local emergency room for injuries he claimed he got in a pit bull attack, but which doctors recognized as mauling by a large mammal. Police ultimately had to rappel down the side of the apartment building and shoot the tiger through a window with a tranquilizer gun. The two apartment dwellers were taken to wildlife refuges far from the big city.

CAT QUOTA RILES MORRISTOWN

2002: In aptly named Morristown, New Jersey, a battle erupted over whether the town has a right to impose a cat quota. After years of bickering, a local dog owner filed a petition with the board of health, complaining that her neighbor  harbored more than a dozen cats whose constant spraying stank up the neighborhood. The cat owner, who in turn filed complaints about the dog's violating her territory, felt the proposed quota of six cats was unfair and that the collaring and tagging requirement posed a health risk to the cats. There was already a law on the town books limiting the number of dogs to five—an ordinance that was instituted in response to excessive barking.

STARVING SNAKES SIZE UP ANGRY LANDLORD

2002: A Houston, Texas, landlord, inspecting one of his rental properties, found that the basement had turned into a reptile house. The tenants he'd recently evicted left behind three Burmese pythons, two yellow anacondas, and three monitor lizards. The reptiles, agitated by their abandonment, struggled with SPCA workers, and one of the huge lizards tore through his transport cage and had to be subdued when he arrived at the animal shelter. No wonder—SPCA officials later determined that the menagerie had not been fed in more than two months.

COUPLE TURNS HOUSE INTO PIGSTY

2002: A big-hearted North Carolina couple who just let "things get away from them" were arrested on animal cruelty charges when deputies found dozens and dozens of potbellied pigs living inside their home. Deputies made the discovery when they went to evict the couple, whose house had been sold in a foreclosure auction. The couple claimed they were rescuing the animals from euthanasia. The pigs were seized and turned over to Animal Haven, a local animal society.

SOMETIMES THE SKY
REALLY IS FALLING . . .

IT'S RAINING— MEAT!

1876: On a cloudless sunny afternoon, a housewife in Bath County, Kentucky, was in her yard making soap when large flakes of raw meat began to fall from the sky. Scientists later identified it as lung tissue, cartilage, and muscle from a horse. They speculated that a flock of vultures disgorged their recent meals all at once while flying over the woman's homestead.

MIND THE RAT

2000s: Over 10 million big brown rats rule London's underground system of sewers, water and electrical conduits, and subway tunnels. They are relative newcomers, emigrants from Russia that overwhelmed the native black rat population in the 18th century. Their capital is in Westminster, which benefits from an abundant flow of refuse from the West End's restaurant district.

Don't forget to take your galoshes: There are also thousands of eels living, loving, and multiplying beneath the city streets.

THREE'S A CROWD

More is not

always merrier—

especially when

disaster strikes.

THE **WRECK**
OF THE **MEDUSA**

1816: Captained by an incompetent and arrogant naval officer, the *Medusa* ran aground on a sandbar 40 miles off the coast of Senegal. The captain,

officers, and upper-class passengers took to the lifeboats. The remaining 150 were crowded onto a makeshift raft and left to fend for themselves in shark-infested waters. Within the first 48 hours there was murder, mutiny, and cannibalism. Rescue came 12 days later—to only 15 survivors. Inquests, trials, and bloody eyewitness accounts of horrors on the raft kept the scandal alive for years.

Silver lining: The incident inspired Theodore Gericault's monumental painting *The Raft of the Medusa,* now in the Louvre.

STUPIDITY
SCORES BIG AT SOCCER STADIUM

February 17, 1974:
In a deadly game of musical chairs, tens of thousands of fans stampeded a sold-out soccer match at Zamalek Stadium in Cairo, Egypt, when they learned there was only one seat for every two tickets sold. (The event was originally scheduled to be held at another stadium that had over 100,000 seats.) Forty-nine would-be spectators died in the melee, and 50 were injured. The promoters later said they had moved the venue to "ensure the comfort of the spectators."

NO JOY IN MUDVILLE

August 15–17, 1969: A new era in the commercialization of music was born when 400,000-plus people gathered on the fields of Max Yasgur's farm in Bethel, New York, to hear more than 32 acts, including the Grateful Dead, Jimi Hendrix, Janis Joplin, and Crosby Stills Nash & Young. Although the three-day festival became a signal event for a generation, the sheer size of the crowd created a disastrous situation: Abandoned cars made roads around Bethel impassable, sanitation at the concert was nil, and plenty of alcohol and drugs sent dozens to the hospital. One man was killed when a tractor rolled over him—the driver did not see him bathing in the mud. The crowd left what had been a beautiful pasture in shambles. When the festival was revived in 1999, there were assaults and rioting in addition to the usual bad trips.

EXCESS OF FAITH KILLS HUNDREDS

1972: Religious faith exceeded common sense as hundreds of enthusiastic Filipino pilgrims crowded a notorious, ancient bridge in Naga City to catch a glimpse of a statue of the Virgin Mary that sailed below it during the Peñafrancia fluvial festival. The bridge, which had collapsed on several occasions and had just undergone repairs, gave way once again, plunging hundreds of spectators into the Bicol River below.

THE ORIGINAL BLACK HOLE OF CALCUTTA

June 20, 1756: The phrase that has become synonymous with dark, filthy, stuffy places had its origin in a rebel insurrection in British-controlled Calcutta. After rebels took control of the city, they imprisoned 64 Britons overnight in a prison cell that was only 18 by 15 feet. The combination of overcrowding and oppressive summer heat killed two thirds of the men by morning. Those who did not die of dehydration, suffocated.

SOMETIMES THE SKY REALLY IS FALLING . . .

CONNECTICUT— THE METEOR MAGNET

On April 8, 1971, a meteorite struck a house in Wethersfield, Connecticut, punching a hole in the roof and damaging furniture. In a bizarre coincidence, on November 8, 1982, a six-pound meteorite crashed through another house in Wethersfield, less than a mile from the first. No one was hurt in either incident.

Look for yourself: The second meteorite is on display at the Peabody Museum at Yale University.

KABOOM!

Explosive situations

and other things

that go boom in

the night—also

in the morning

FIREBALL EXPLODES OVER NORTHERN SIBERIA

June 30, 1908: With a force estimated at 2000 times that of the Hiroshima bomb, an unidentified cosmic object exploded over the Tunguska region of northern Siberia, flattening a forest over half the size of Rhode Island. The thunderous explosion was heard more than 500 miles away. Animals standing in fields over eight miles beyond the blast zone were knocked over. No one was killed, but it was a bad day for pine trees.

HAVOC
IN HALIFAX HARBOR

1917: On the morning of December 6, a Belgian steamer plowed into the *Mont Blanc,* a heavily loaded munitions ship entering Halifax harbor. The resulting fire soon ignited 8 million tons of TNT aboard the *Mont Blanc.* The blast leveled 2½ square miles of neighboring towns, whose residents thought they had been hit by a German air raid or an earthquake. A tidal wave in the harbor damaged dozens of ships moored at the docks and fortuitously flooded an adjacent munitions dump, where thousands of tons of explosives lay in the path of the raging fire. Because the explosion occurred during World War I, there was a news and investigative blackout.

NAPOLEON'S
GUTS NO MATCH FOR
LUFTWAFFE

1941: After death, the very famous are often immortalized in songs or stories—or big jars in museum cabinets. The pickled intestines of Napoleon Bonaparte were a prized possession of the Hunterian Collection in London's Royal College of Surgeons. The Little Colonel's innards, along with the college itself, went up in smoke during the London Blitz of 1941.

HOUSEWIFE OVERCHARGED FOR PRODUCE

2003: A woman in Trieste, Italy, got the shock of her life when the artichoke she was peeling gave off sparks and blew up in her hands. She immediately called police, who took the 'choke's remains into custody. A terrorist in Northern Italy had been planting explosives in supermarkets over the past ten years, but this was not his handiwork. No traces of explosive were found on the artichoke, leaving no explanation for the violence-prone vegetable.

Three Blasts for the Record Books

- The loudest noise ever heard by mankind occurred when the Krakatoa volcano exploded on August 26, 1883. The sound could be heard 3,000 miles away. Tsunamis scoured neighboring shores, killing at least 36,000 people. Five cubic miles of rock and ash were thrown thousands of feet into the atmosphere, and the sky turned dark across a 100-mile radius.

- The biggest single man-made explosion before the atomic blast at Hiroshima took place at the Royal Air Force bomb depot in Fauld, Hanbury, England, a mine that had been converted into a bomb dump and repair station. On November 27, 1944, a 1,000-pound bomb exploded while its detonator was being repaired, setting off a chain reaction explosion of 4,000 tons of bombs and killing 68 people. The soil was blasted into the sky and landed as far as 11 miles away, opening a crater 1,000 by 300 yards.

- The biggest boom felt by the most people was the explosion of the catalyst reactor at the Humble Oil and Refining Company in Linden, New Jersey, at 11 P.M. on December 5, 1970. The refinery was located one mile west of Arthur Kill, the body of water that separates New Jersey and Staten Island, New York. Windows were shattered all over Staten Island and as far away as Elizabeth, New Jersey, where looters took advantage of the windowless stores. The resulting fireball filled the sky, inspiring witnesses to compare it to a scene out of hell. More than 13 million people in a 40-mile radius felt the blast. There were a few dozen injuries, but, miraculously, no one was killed.

***MAKING THE BEST OF A BAD SITUATION:
THE SHOW MUST GO ON***

CONEY ISLAND'S DREAMLAND BURNS DOWN

May 27, 1911: On the eve of the season's opening day, exploding lightbulbs in the Hell Gate attraction at the Coney Island amusement park ignited a pool of tar on the floor. Hell Gate burst into flames that spread and consumed the entire park, whose confectionery façades were made of highly flammable lath and plaster.

"Burned out but still doing business": The freak show and some of the other sideshow attractions set up in tents on the smoldering ruins.

BLITZED LONDONER BLAMES SELF FOR HOME GOING DOWN THE DRAIN

1944: After a German air raid destroyed a house in London, rescuers cleared the debris to find an old man, naked and miraculously unhurt, in his bathtub. The survivor lamented, "I don't know how it happened. I just pulled out the plug and the house blew up."

THE QUICK AND THE DEAD

Life does not cease to be funny when people die any more than it ceases to be serious when people laugh.

—GEORGE BERNARD SHAW

PROFIT OF DOOM

January 4, 1937: After a nasty motorcycle accident, Angelo Hays was declared dead and was buried three days later. Two days after the burial he was exhumed at the insistence of insurance investigators, who needed to know the exact cause of his death. When they put him on the autopsy table, the pathologist discovered that Hays was still breathing.

Hays completely recovered and later became a celebrity when he began touring France with a "security coffin," which was outfitted with food, an air line, and a communications channel in case someone was buried alive. He even made live appearances from inside the contraption on European television.

DEAD WIFE BECOMES DENTAL ASSISTANT

1775: A London dentist, Martin van Butchell, intent on keeping his practice in the public eye, embalmed his dead wife and put her on display in the parlor. Many came to see the macabre missus, but when he remarried, his new wife made him send the old one to a museum, where she remained until 1941, when the building was incinerated by German bombs.

———

LIFESTYLES OF THE LIVING DEAD, PART I

2003: An elderly Chilean man returned from a trip to find that his wife was gone, his house had been sold, and he had been declared dead. Even his personal effects were nowhere to be found. The man could not believe that his house, which he co-owned, had been allowed to change hands without a proper death certificate. At last report, police were still investigating.

WOMAN DECLARED DEAD; DEAD WOMAN DISAGREES

Summer 1915: The first funeral of a South Carolina woman ended in fright and mayhem when her sister arrived late to the funeral and begged to see her sibling one last time. The minister assented, even though the coffin was already six feet under. When they pried the lid off, the "deceased" sat up in her coffin and greeted her sister, scattering mourners and the shocked clergyman. It turned out that the 30-year-old epileptic had been prematurely declared dead after a seizure.

The woman's second funeral was not held until 40 years later.

HANDSOME RANSOM DEMANDED FOR CHAPLIN CORPSE

1977: After Charlie Chaplin was buried on December 27, he enjoyed only two months of blessed rest before two Eastern European thieves dug him up and demanded a $600,000 ransom for his return. His widow, Oona, refused to pay it. Police soon found the robbers and then Charlie, whom they had buried in a cornfield about ten miles from his original resting place at Corsier-sur-Vevey, Switzerland. Chaplin was reinterred in May 1978, this time in a concrete vault.

LIFESTYLES OF THE LIVING DEAD, PART II

2003: The unscrupulous and greedy in India have had a field day in recent years by using fake death certificates to seize the property of living relatives. Despite many appeals of the "living dead," the revenue offices that keep the records refuse to reinstate them to the rolls of the living so they can reclaim their property. Protests have been organized to force the state to do something for more than 35,000 walking, talking "corpses"—one group recently held a Hindu last-rites ceremony on the steps of the state assembly building.

Death Certificate

Extra extra read all about it. This document certifies that _____ and _____ were joined in holy matrimony in front of God and in a State of intoxication on this day _____. May God have mercies upon your souls. Now this is just filler material here because I have no idea what one of these things look like _____ that was a good place to put blank space.

Signed _____   Bride _____

Groom _____   Witness _____

Witness _____

DEAD MAN GROWS MUSTACHE, INCHES, FOR OWN FUNERAL

2002: A Romanian family was surprised to learn that their dead relative not only sported a new mustache for his funeral but was also a few inches taller.

Despite the funeral director's insistence that a body can change after death, the distraught relatives, recognizing the right clothes on the wrong body, postponed the funeral. After he died at home, the deceased had been sent to the morgue for an autopsy, where his corpse had been mixed up with a similar one taken to the medical examiner's office on the same day. The right corpse was eventually found and buried, and the family made plans to bury the morgue in a lawsuit.

MOTORISTS FACE STIFF LINES

2003: Gasoline became so scarce in Zimbabwe that people were playing dead to get it. Several establishments let families on the way to funerals cut ahead in the long lines. People were showing up at gas stations with coffins in tow. The police arrested several mortuary workers for renting corpses to motorists who liked to go the extra mile.

FLYNN'S PICKLED PAL

1942: Actor and legendary imbiber Errol Flynn flew out of his Hollywood home after he found his drinking buddy John Barrymore sitting in his living room—because Flynn knew the actor was dead. Flynn's pals were howling outside. They had borrowed Barrymore's body from the mortuary for a final performance—one that Barrymore himself would have appreciated.

HOPE BURIED ALIVE BY NEWS ORGANIZATION

June 5, 1998: Associated Press accidentally ran an obituary of Bob Hope on its website on June 5, 1998, prompting members of Congress to memorialize him on Capitol Hill. The news began breaking over the radio before Hope's publicist could assure the nation that Hope, then 95, was alive and well.

Hope passed his hundredth birthday before he really died on July 27, 2003.

WIVES WORTH MORE DEAD THAN ALIVE

2002: Police broke up a Chinese syndicate that was digging up female corpses from cemeteries and selling them to families of dead bachelors. These dead brides were then "married" to the deceased single men, so that they could rest peacefully in the spirit world. Some things never change: The corpses ranged in age from 18 to 72— the younger ones were more expensive.

———

LIFESTYLES OF THE LIVING DEAD, PART III

2003: An Argentinean man discovered he'd been living on borrowed time when he was refused treatment for a toothache at a local hospital. Medical records indicated that he'd been dead for more than 20 years. Hospital officials produced his death certificate, which stated that he died in 1980. Meanwhile the shocking news made the toothache go away.

Not Dead Yet

Hope was not the only one to be eulogized before his time:

- Jerry Mathers, Beaver Cleaver on the original *Leave It to Beaver* series, was rumored to be dead in 1969 after a soldier with the same name died in Vietnam.

- Kurt Cobain, lead singer of Nirvana, was declared dead of a drug overdose by CNN in March 1994. He really died a month later when he shot himself.

- Joe DiMaggio was nearly, but not quite, dead when NBC reported that he had passed on January 24, 1999. He died later that year, on March 8.

- *People* magazine reported that actor Abe Vigoda died in 1982, prompting the undead actor to pose for a photo of himself reading his own obituary. Vigoda's life status can be monitored 24/7 on his website, www.abevigoda.com.

- The publication of Mark Twain's obituary in the *New York Journal* on June 2, 1897, inspired him to coin the now famous quip, "The reports of my death are greatly exaggerated."

ANCIENT GREEK
DECLARED
DEAD

2002: When a proud Greek grandfather, looking forward to voting for his grandson in a local election on his island home of Melissourgoi, went to check the voter registry lists, he discovered that local officials had left him off because they assumed he was dead. To save time, the election officials eliminated anyone on the list born before 1890, presuming that they could no longer be alive. The enraged 113-year-old man demanded and got an apology and reinstatement of his voter status.

SCHOOL'S OUT

Sometimes college

is even more

of a blast than

students anticipated.

"CRACKER"
CRACKS
UP HALLOWED HALL

1814: Students in the 19th century didn't have the Internet and had to resort to much cruder devices with which to wreak havoc. On January 14, 1814, students at Princeton University stuffed a hollow log with two pounds of gunpowder, placed the "Big 'Cracker" in the entranceway to historic Nassau Hall, and let the big firecracker blow. The huge explosion blew out the hall's windows and cracked many of the walls. No one was killed, but the university's dogged pursuit of the perpetrators led to a series of expulsions, court trials, protests, more explosions, and more expulsions that continued for years.

EXPLOSIVE WRITER GETS BAD REVIEW

1806: James Fenimore Cooper, author of *The Last of the Mohicans* and other novels of the frontier, was thoroughly familiar with the many uses of gunpowder. During his junior year at Yale, he pushed a rag loaded with the stuff through the keyhole of a friend's room and lit it. The resulting explosion got Cooper, a known prankster, expelled.

CORNELL STUDENTS PASS GAS

February 1894: The most notorious and deadly college prank of the 19th century began with a riot, when members of the sophomore class at Cornell University tried to keep the freshman class from entering the hall where their class banquet was being held. When the freshman banquet finally did start, the sophomores drilled a hole into the kitchen, thinking it was the dining hall, and pumped it full of chlorine gas. Several waiters passed out and the cook died. A grand jury was convened in Ithaca, but there was insufficient evidence to press charges.

PRINCETON EXPELS
ONE THIRD OF
STUDENT BODY

1807: College campuses have always been hotbeds of rebellion, and in 1807 Princeton University was forced to expel 68 of its 200 students for insubordination. The incident began when three students were expelled for insulting a college officer. The student government appealed for their reinstatement, but the administration responded by calling a collegewide meeting at which each student would be called to pledge obedience to the rules of the school. The students rioted instead.

MORNINGSIDE HEIGHTS REACHES NEW LOW

1968: Columbia students, upset with the university's policing of on-campus demonstrations, stormed the president's office, took three administrators hostage,

and eventually occupied five university buildings. They refused to end the siege until they were guaranteed amnesty for their actions.

After a five-day standoff, the university sent in 1,000 police. Hundreds were arrested, 130 were injured, and the alienation of the student body only increased.

MIXED DRINKS

The consequences

of having one too

many, especially if

you're an elephant

WE WHO ARE ABOUT TO DIE SALUD YOU . . .

1972: Guests at a wedding in New Delhi, India, were treated to bootleg liquor that had been juiced up with wood alcohol and varnish. Hundreds became ill and more than 100 died.

When police tracked down the bootlegger, he was found dead, along with his mother and brother. They had all attended the wedding.

GONE TO THE DOGS

1999: One unfortunate South African got so drunk that he was unable to run away from a pack of wild dogs that accosted him and a friend when they were walking home late one night. The friend escaped with only a bite on the leg, while the man not only succumbed to the savage dogs but was then dragged away and eaten by ravenous pigs, which had finished off half of him by the next morning.

PINK ELEPHANTS RUN AMOK IN INDIA

1999: Human encroachment on the forests of Assam Province, India, has resulted in more frequent wild-elephant attacks. Throw man's vices into the mix and you get a real disaster: A herd of 15 elephants wandered into a village in northeastern Assam and happened upon huts filled with casks of rice beer. They drank the beer, became inebriated, and went on a deadly rampage—killing four, injuring six, and tearing apart the village and nearby rice paddies.

SWEDEN WAITS FOR ANIMALS TO SOBER UP

2003: Thousands of waxwing birds in Sweden feasted on fermenting rowanberries, got drunk, and flew into large plate-glass windows at Karlstad University, leaving the windows intact but killing themselves. Officials at the university said all they could do was wait until all the wild berries had been eaten.

Elsewhere in Sweden, police had to kill a drunken elk that was chasing a boy—the animal became intoxicated after eating fermented apples on the forest floor.

OVERZEALOUS

Doing too good a job

does not always

lead to better

circumstances.

MAN SMOKES OUT WASPS, SELF

2003: A Croatian man who found a wasp's nest lodged in his living-room window decided to smoke the pests out. But he poured so much gasoline on the nest that when he lit it, he also torched the window, the house, and himself.

GREEDY PROSPECTORS DIG OWN GRAVE

1955: After a large nugget of gold was found in the state of Minas Gerais, Brazil, prospectors gathered and began to dig for the mother lode. Finding nothing, they dug deeper and deeper, until they were 40 feet below the surface, whereupon the trench they were standing in collapsed and they were buried alive.

VENDING MACHINE RETALIATES

2003: A German man landed in the hospital with cuts and bruises after a cigarette vending machine fell on him. When the machine failed to deliver his pack, the zealous smoker attacked it with such force that he brought it, along with much of the wall behind, down on his head.

THINK BEFORE YOU ROCK

1995: Since common sense does not always prevail, in 1995 the Consumer Product Safety Commission found it necessary to put labels on soda-can vending machines, warning people that rocking the machine, a popular maneuver to obtain free sodas, can result in serious injury or death. Between 1978 and 1995, 37 deaths and 113 injuries resulted from machines that overturned on thrifty customers.

MAN EXTERMINATES PEST, HOUSE

2003: An overzealous homeowner in India was not satisfied with trapping a mouse—he wanted to make sure it didn't come back, so he tied a kerosene-laden cloth around its tail and lit it. The mouse escaped with the flaming cloth and set fire to the house, which burned to the ground.

DEER CAUGHT IN THE HEADLIGHTS

See what happens when

the mesmerized, the foolish,

and the too damned curious

won't get out of the way.

WEATHERMAN OVERESTIMATES SELF, UNDERESTIMATES STORM

September 8, 1900: Overconfidence on the part of the weather bureau and Galveston's weather officer, Isaac Cline, led to one of the worst hurricane death tolls in U.S. history. The Texas bureau failed to heed warnings of forecasters in Cuba, which was being battered by the worst hurricane ever. Cline's own analysis of Galveston's topography convinced him that the city  could weather even a bad storm. As a result, children frolicked on the beach with their parents as the waves grew higher and higher. Eventually the storm engulfed the entire city, killing more than 6,000 people.

VOLCANO UNIMPRESSED BY PRAYERS

March 20, 1963: Despite witnessing weeks of rumbling and brimstone belching, thousands of worshippers, whose faith exceeded their

common sense, gathered on the eastern slope of Mount Agung to celebrate the sacred Balinese Eka Dasa Rudra festival with chants and prayers. The volcano, apparently unimpressed, blew its top, killing hundreds of worshippers in midprayer. The spewing rocks, ash, lava, and poisonous gas destroyed everything within a ten-mile radius and left more than 80,000 Balinese homeless.

POKÉMON SEIZES CAPTIVE AUDIENCE

1997: By 1999, parents all over America were having fits over Pokémon, but in December two years prior, the popular children's cartoon caused actual seizures in almost 700 Japanese children. The offending episode featured two Pokémon characters fighting in front of a flashing, abstract background. The frequency of the flashing is thought to have triggered the epileptic reaction. The show was immediately pulled from Japanese television for evaluation, and when it premiered in the United States a year later, the troublesome scenes had been modified. Physicians later concluded that only a fraction of the children affected had true photosensitive epilepsy.

PLAGUE OF SNAKES PRECEDES VOLCANIC EXPLOSION

May 8, 1902: In the month before Mount Pelée in Martinique exploded, the mountain began shaking and belching ash and sulfur. The disturbance caused more than 100 six-foot-long fer-de-lance snakes to leave their mountain dens and invade the city of Saint-Pierre. They killed 50 people and numerous animals before giant street cats ate them. Despite the rumblings and the plague of biblical proportions, the citizens did not take the volcano seriously enough. When Pelée erupted on May 8, it obliterated the

entire city in three minutes, destroyed 18 ships in the harbor, and killed nearly 30,000 people.

ALIEN ENCOUNTERS

Being a stranger in a

strange land is not

always easy . . .

CITY HIPSTER GETS ROCKED BY LOCALS

2002: An Austrian man who stopped to visit his father in a Turkish village got a rude greeting. Unfortunately, he had bright red hair, was wearing all black, and sported piercings all over his face. The villagers thought he was a Satanist or an alien from another planet— and stoned him.

DOUBLE WHAMMY ON DARK ROAD

2002: On a very dark and isolated country road in Iowa, a hit-and-run driver killed two people. When police arrived to investigate the crime scene, they ran over the bodies again.

CURIOUS FISHERMEN COME FACE-TO-FACE WITH MONSTER

April 1875: While investigating a large, shapeless mass floating in the sea near Inishbofin Island, three Irish fishermen were surprised to discover it was a 40-foot giant squid. It sprayed them with ink and almost capsized their boat when it began thrashing around in the water. Rather than being suitably impressed by the rare spectacle, they hacked the squid apart, tentacle by tentacle, and then dragged the whole mess back to shore.

THAT OLD BLACK MAGIC

2002: Police in North London raided a market that supplied "bush meat" to African shops throughout the city. The victuals, which included bush rats, giant African snails, and a smoked crocodile head (the Viagra of the African jungle), are used in black-magic rituals. Not only is bush-meat trafficking illegal, but much of the meat had turned rancid long before it reached Britain and, if eaten, would have been a threat to public health.

SPACE INVADERS

These immigrants from the animal kingdom just want their piece of the pie—sometimes literally.

RATS ARE KINGS IN QUEENS

2003: Rats as big as cats forced a Queens, New York, firehouse to temporarily shut down so that its walls could be gutted. Many rats went merrily about their business in defiance of exterminators, moving into ceilings and other crevasses; those that succumbed to the exterminators' weapons made the firehouse uninhabitable with their putrid odor.

MOUSE MAKES CHICKEN OF DINER

2003: A diner, biting into a piece of his fried-chicken combo, was revolted to discover that it was actually a fried mouse. It turned out that Baltimore health officials had closed the place twice before for infestation.

BEES HOLD FAMILY HOSTAGE FOR 48 HOURS

1998: A swarm of 20,000 bees descended on a family's house in Dorset, England, making a frightful buzzing sound and crawling all over the windows, doors, and chimneys. The terrified mother, trapped inside with her two children, called the RSPCA, the police, and the fire brigade. They all came out to inspect the situation, only to say they couldn't do anything because bees are a protected species in the UK. They suggested she call a beekeeper. The woman was worried she'd never find a solution when, on the third day, the horde departed as unexpectedly as they had arrived.

LOCUSTS LEAVE LITTLE LEFTOVER

Summer 1874: In a plague of biblical proportions, a black cloud of locusts 120 billion strong swept over the Great Plains. They destroyed the corn and wheat, vacuumed up all produce on the vines and in the fields, and bored into the ground, eating bulbs and root vegetables. Then they attacked trees and wood fences, leather harnesses, furniture, curtains, and the clothing on people's backs. Local livestock were delighted to gorge themselves on the locusts—with dire consequences. Poultry ate them and fell down sick; pigs that consumed them took on their flavor, making their meat inedible. Trains almost derailed on tracks slick with locust excrement and carcasses. The devastation recurred during the next three summers—but in 1877 the locusts seem to have spent themselves and have never again appeared on such a scale.

CATERPILLARS CREEP OUT LONDON BUSINESS

2002: In a scene straight out of a 1950s science-fiction movie, a building in London had to be evacuated when thousands of poisonous moth caterpillars covered the office windows. The big, hairy, wart-covered caterpillars caused severe skin irritation to anyone they touched. The area around the building was cordoned off, and exterminators dressed in space suits fumigated the building and its environs. The caterpillars had been feeding in nearby bushes, awaiting their pupa stage. Office workers who were allowed back into the building were told to keep the windows closed to prevent reinfestation.

SOMETIMES THE SKY REALLY IS FALLING . . .

IT'S RAINING— NONDAIRY CREAMER!

1969: The Borden Company in Chester, South Carolina, had a problem with its exhaust vents. Whenever they clogged, Cremora, the powdered nondairy creamer, spewed into the air and dusted the entire town. The powder was not toxic, but it created a sticky mess whenever it rained. "It looks like you haven't washed your windows for a hundred years," one local resident complained.

SNAKEHEADS DEVOUR THE COMPETITION

2002: Two imported northern snakehead fish were dumped in a pond in Maryland, where they multiplied with abandon. They ate up almost all the native fish, necessitating the poisoning of the entire pond to prevent their spread into other Maryland waterways. The federal government has proposed a ban on the importation of snakeheads, due to this and other "invasions" that have cost taxpayers millions of dollars.

TERMITES CUT OUT MIDDLEMAN

2003: Termites in the Shenzhen province of China saved one man the trouble of wasting his money on an exterminator— they ate the money themselves. When the man, who'd used his mattress as a piggy bank, went to retrieve his cash, he discovered that termites had consumed almost half his savings.

CAST OF HAIRY EXTRAS UPSTAGES STARS

July 2002: Record drought conditions forced Los Angeles rats from their homes in the dense park foliage and into the sun-and-sand splendor of the Santa Monica strip, where six restaurants were temporarily forced to close. Rats were also found basking by swimming pools in Beverly Hills and Pacific Palisades, after gorging on flowers, garden vegetables, and food left outside by unsuspecting homeowners. The invasion caused usually environmentally conscious Californians to reexamine their priorities and call in exterminators. Said one resident, "We're very conscientious, but we hate rats."

UP IN SMOKE

Colossal

conflagrations from

the history books

CURSES, BROILED AGAIN!

1657: The long-sleeved robes worn by a temple attendant were blamed for a two-day fire that devastated Tokyo and killed more than 100,000 residents. The fire started during an exorcism in the Honmyoji Temple, when sparks from the ceremonial burning of a cursed kimono ignited an attendant's robe, which in turn set the whole temple ablaze. High winds whipped the temple fire into a massive wall of flames that consumed the mostly wooden city.

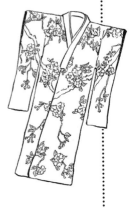

BOVINE INTERVENTION

October 8–10, 1871:
Whatever the exact role
of Mrs. O'Leary's cow,
Chicago was an accident
waiting to happen, thanks
to its mazes of wooden
buildings and an exceptionally dry
summer. The fire began on October 8 in
a crowded tenement, jumped to St. Paul's
Catholic Church, and thanks to strong
winds, quickly fanned out across the city.
Fighting it with water was almost useless,
mostly because the pumps used weren't very
powerful and there wasn't enough water
reserved for firefighting. The fire largely
burned out on its own two days later. As in
London two centuries before, the fire wiped
out a crowded rabbit warren of buildings.
Chicago was rebuilt within a few years and, as
a result of the city's total destruction, led the
way in modern architecture and city planning.

LUMINARIES CAUGHT IN HISTORIC MELTDOWN

1932: The wax figures of Julius Caesar, Henry VIII, Leon Trotsky, and Charles Lindbergh all went up in smoke when the Eden Musée in Coney Island burned down. Like the more famous Madame Tussauds, the Eden Musée housed historical dioramas rendered in wax, as well as a chamber of horrors. Wax portraits that didn't melt completely were otherwise damaged. In the case of Marie Antoinette, history repeated itself—the wax statue was decapitated, just like the real queen.

WATER EVERYWHERE, BUT NOT A DROP FOR CONFLAGRATION

October 5, 1858: America's first world's fair was held in the Crystal Palace, a grand domed greenhouse erected in 1853 on what is now Bryant Park in New York City. Just five years later, an arsonist set fire to the building. Miraculously, the 2,000 people inside the glass-and-steel structure got out safely. The building was reduced to rubble in just 30 minutes, despite being adjacent to New York's main water reservoir. Firefighting equipment was too primitive to make a difference.

CRASSUS RUNS ROMAN FIRE SALE

First century B.C.: Until A.D. 6, there was no fire department in ancient Rome. Fighting fires was a private affair and was usually handled by slaves. In the early first century B.C., the corrupt Roman general Crassus took

lucrative advantage of this—he'd show up at neighborhood fires (some of which his henchmen set) and offer to buy the burning property from the distraught owner, with the price declining as the conflagration grew. Only when the owner relented did Crassus send in his team to quench the flames.

I sometimes wonder if the manufacturers of foolproof items keep a fool or two on their payroll to test things.

—ALAN COREN

TRAGEDY PLAYS IN FIREPROOF THEATER

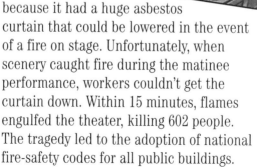

December 30, 1903: The owners of the brand-new Iroquois Theater in Chicago bragged that it was "absolutely fireproof" because it had a huge asbestos curtain that could be lowered in the event of a fire on stage. Unfortunately, when scenery caught fire during the matinee performance, workers couldn't get the curtain down. Within 15 minutes, flames engulfed the theater, killing 602 people. The tragedy led to the adoption of national fire-safety codes for all public buildings.

ELEGANT HOTEL'S HOSPITALITY GOES UP IN SMOKE

1883: Although fire and insurance companies refused to insure the structure because they deemed it too dangerous, the Newhall House Hotel, the "most elegant hotel in Milwaukee," stayed in business without bothering to fix its fire escapes. Sure enough, at 3 A.M. on January 10, the place caught fire. Like the *Titanic*'s passengers, most of the guests were not immediately awakened because hotel management thought they could easily douse the blaze. Dozens died as the hotel burned to the ground.

BITING THE HAND THAT FEEDS YOU

Ingrates of every

species turn on

those who love

them most.

PYTHON KILLS OWNER, THEN TURNS ON FIREMAN

2002: After removing his pet snake from his cage and wrapping it around his neck, a Colorado man was strangled by the 10-foot-long, 80-pound Burmese python he had raised from babyhood. Five police and firemen were ultimately needed to pull the snake off. The snake then turned on one of the rescuers, knocked him to the ground, coiled itself around his arm, and began dragging him across the room. The fireman managed, with the help of his colleagues, to wrestle the snake back into its cage.

Some people never learn: The deceased had been convicted three years earlier of violating city code by keeping a snake that was more than six feet long and had been told to get rid of the reptile.

I AM SIAMESE, IF YOU DON'T PLEASE

2002: A seriously disgruntled Siamese cat, which had attacked a babysitter earlier in the afternoon, turned on its own family, tearing their clothes and clawing their flesh until they were forced to run outside and call the police. Unaccustomed to confronting a mad cat, the police had to improvise. They used a blanket and hamper to subdue the feline, which they then locked inside a pet carrier and transported directly to a veterinarian.

PET OWNERS IN TIGHT SQUEEZE

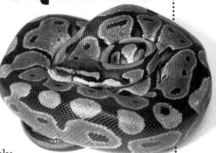

2002: A mother and daughter in Utah, who gave free rein in their apartment to their six-foot-long African rock python, paid dearly when the snake thanked them by giving the daughter a really tight hug around the head. The ungrateful reptile then thwarted the mother's attempts to free the girl by trapping mom's arm. The police were called, and after kicking down the front door, they were able to pry the snake off the shaken pair and cart it away to an animal shelter.

FAT CAT TURNS MAUL RAT

2000: A fund-raiser at Zoo Boise, in Idaho, ended badly when a 700-pound Amur tiger attacked a woman attending the event. The ungrateful recipient of the charity's largesse escaped from his cage while a group from the "Feast for the Beast" dinner was being given a tour of the tiger house. The tiger knocked the woman down and mauled her, breaking her leg and leaving her with several lacerations and puncture wounds. She was taken to a local hospital. The tiger managed to save his own life by retreating into his cage before security personnel arrived.

VIPER BITES THE HAND THAT FEEDS HIM

2000: A Buffalo, New York, man landed in the hospital in critical condition after his highly poisonous West African gaboon viper bit him. In order to save him, antivenom had to be rushed to Buffalo from the Bronx Zoo. Turns out the man had a whole menagerie of potentially deadly reptiles, including a cobra, a rattlesnake, and a 200-pound alligator named Albert.

Once discovered, poor Albert, who had previously had his run of the house, was "depetted"—sent, that is, to the Buffalo Zoo.

FROM LITTLE ACORNS GROW MIGHTY OAKS . . .

Lt. Del Teagan, alligator specialist with the Florida Fish and Wildlife Conservation Commission, on why stupid pet owners should think twice before bringing a three-inch alligator into their homes:

"When they weigh 600 pounds and eat your dog for lunch, they're not so cute anymore."

SURPRISING METAMORPHOSIS LEADS TO NASTY BITE

2001: A London man and his son didn't realize what they'd gotten themselves into when the son brought a two-inch lizard home from a pet swap. Despite being fed nothing but fried fish for 18 months, the lizard grew into a 2½-foot monster. After it bit the father, the boy called the RSPCA, who identified the "lizard" as a spectacled caiman, which routinely grow to be seven feet long. The caiman was taken to a sanctuary, where he recovered from his bad English diet.

MAN IS HIS OWN LAST MEAL

January 2000: A 56-year-old lawyer from Naples, Italy, was found dead in his home—eaten by his pet lion. His remains were found in the lion's cage. Investigators were unsure if the lion attacked and ate its owner, or if the man died of natural causes and was consumed when the lion got hungry.

IRONY IN ACTION

A man shoots a giant cactus,

which falls on his head;

a gun kills a gun maker;

an unfortunate man loses

his hand in a tug-of-war:

kind of makes sense,

in a weird way.

PIG KILLS PIG SLAUGHTERER

2002: What comes around goes around—at a slaughterhouse in Minnesota, a pig that had just been shot fell on a rifle, which went off and killed a slaughter man standing nearby.

WEATHER OBSERVER EXPERIENCES TOO MUCH WEATHER

2001: The National Weather Service lost one of its observers in Sledge, Mississippi, when the woman—who was paid to measure rainfall but not trained to spot severe storms—was killed by a tornado that destroyed her home.

GUNSLINGER DUELS WITH CACTUS, LOSES

1982: In a scene straight out of a Wile E. Coyote cartoon, a man in the desert outside Phoenix, Arizona, fired two rounds from his shotgun into a giant 40-foot-tall saguaro cactus. A 23-foot section above the blasts broke off and fell right on top of the man, crushing him to death.

BOOKS KEEP TEACHER IN DETENTION

2003: A shelf loaded with heavy books collapsed, trapping a 60-year-old Croatian math teacher in his bed for three days. The shaken but uninjured man was finally discovered after his wife, who was in the hospital, called the police when her husband failed to show up for his usual visits.

———

GUN KILLS GUN MAKER

1929: B. V. Vickers, a British arms manufacturer, was killed during a hunting trip when his dog lunged at the man who was loading Vickers's gun, which then accidentally discharged, giving the gun maker a taste of his own, uh, armaments.

FEAR OF FLYING LEADS TO FEARFUL FLIGHT

2003: An Australian man decided to cure his fear of flying by making a parachute jump. But when he and his instructor jumped, their harness strap caught on the plane's steps, leaving them dangling upside down thousands of feet in the air. The pilot was able to cut them loose to finish their drop.

MAN TORN BY TEAM LOYALTY

May 1997: A Chattanooga, Tennessee, man served as his team's anchor during a tug-of-war game at his company picnic. Standing last in a line of 25, he wrapped the rope tightly around his wrist. When the other team gave it their all, his hand ripped right off.

SHARK DISAGREES WITH SHARK EXPERT

2002: A shark expert—described by a former colleague as an "accident waiting to happen"—was badly bitten by a 350-pound shark while filming a TV special in the Bahamas. The scientist had been standing in cloudy water with several sharks, watching as they chased their prey, when one chomped right through his leg, severing arteries and destroying tissue.

Shark researchers had questioned the man's actions for years and claimed that he used unorthodox and dangerous methods they did not endorse and that he was deluding himself by thinking he could read sharks' minds and elude attack.

SICILIAN MAN ADMIRES OWN TOMB TOO CLOSELY

2001: A 63-year-old retired Sicilian man with time on his hands took to regularly inspecting the progress of his family tomb. During his last visit to the marble structure, he fell off the ladder he was using to get a better look at the construction. He struck his head on a stone step and was killed instantly.

MAKING THE BEST OF A BAD SITUATION: SURVIVOR'S PRIDE

BROOK WATSON ATTACKED BY SHARK

1749: While serving as a crewmember on a merchant ship, Brook Watson, age 14, was attacked by a shark as he swam in Havana harbor. His shipmates beat the shark off, but not before it had taken Watson's right leg with it.

Watson recovered and went on to become a successful merchant and lord mayor of London, despite a political opponent's assertion that the shark would have done better to bite off Watson's other end, as a wooden head would have served him better than what he had.

Watson used an emblem of his amputated leg on his coat of arms.

LIFE FINALLY IMITATES ART

Dying is the most embarrassing thing that can ever happen to you, because someone's got to take care of all your details.

—ANDY WARHOL

1987: All his life, Andy Warhol had a terrible fear of hospitals and waited until he was in excruciating pain before consenting to a much-needed gall bladder operation. The surgery was successful, but by 6:30 the next morning, he was dead.

Nothing to Fear but Fear Itself

Warhol was not the only one with a seemingly irrational fear that later figured in his death:

- Composer Arnold Schoenberg feared the number 13. He died on Friday, the 13th of July, at 13 minutes to midnight, 1951.

- Singer Richie Valens had a fear of airplanes. He died in the same plane crash that killed Buddy Holly and the Big Bopper on February 3, 1959.

- Actress Natalie Wood had a fear of water. She drowned when she fell off a boat on November 29, 1981.

SNAKE CHARMER FAILS TO CHARM SNAKE

1999: A local snake charmer in Thailand, famed for his snake-catching skills, was summoned to catch a python that had broken into a home in his village. After bagging the snake, he headed home and was approached by villagers who asked to see the snake. He pulled it out of the bag and proudly draped it around his neck. The python choked him to death on the spot.

SURPRISING DISCOVERIES

*You never know
what you might find
when you investigate
a crime scene, clean
out an apartment,
or open the grave
of a loved one . . .*

SHOW ME THE MONKEY!

2002: Wildlife smuggling supplies the second most lucrative black market worldwide, after gunrunning. Due to increased security checks at airports, officials are now finding more animals hidden in baggage or even on the smugglers themselves. Some customs inspectors at L.A. International got a wild surprise when they opened a suitcase and a bird of paradise flew out. When questioned, the suitcase's owner revealed that he also had a pair of monkeys in his pants.

STAR'S UNTIMELY MURDER LEADS TO PORNO CACHE

June 29, 1978: After Bob Crane, star of the 1960s sitcom *Hogan's Heroes,* was found bludgeoned to death in his hotel apartment in Scottsdale, Arizona, police uncovered the actor's less-than-wholesome hobby of making homemade sex videos. Professional equipment and more than 50 videotapes were found in the apartment, confirming rumors that had been making it hard for Crane to get work.

Although Crane's killer throttled him with a video cord, investigators were unable to connect anyone in the videos to his murder, which remains unsolved.

Crane's life became the subject of the 2002 movie *Auto Focus.*

TUPPERWARE PARTY?

2002: Police called to the home of a University of Florida professor on a domestic battery complaint made two interesting discoveries—a cache of guns, including military-grade weapons and ammunition, and more than a dozen heads, limbs, and other body parts stored in Tupperware containers in the refrigerator. The specimens belonged to the university, where the professor taught neuroanatomy. He claimed he was conducting research, even though he didn't have authorization from the college to remove the specimens from the lab. The university promptly fired him, and the army had to be called in to remove the heavy weapons.

WIFE DISCOVERS ANOTHER WOMAN IN HUSBAND'S TOMB

1978: When her husband's grave was opened so that his body could be moved to a different plot, a Rhode Island woman was horrified to discover the body of a woman in his place. His body was eventually found in another plot, and the woman, who had been praying for the soul of her spouse in the wrong spot for 17 years, filed a $125,000 lawsuit.

———

THE WRECK OF THE BATAVIA

1629: When the merchant ship *Batavia* foundered off the coast of Australia, its passengers thought their luck had changed when they sighted land. Instead they found an island refuge inhabited by mutineers who had long been stranded there. Before help arrived, the mutineers murdered more than 100 of the *Batavia*'s 360 passengers.

LOCAL HOBO SECURES WORK IN PERMANENT ART COLLECTION

2002: After English painter Robert Lenkiewicz died, a gruesome discovery came to light in his studio—the embalmed body of a local tramp who had died almost 20 years earlier. The artist had been using him as a model, both before and after death. The vagrant, Edwin Mackenzie, whose residence was a barrel at the time he first met the artist, had requested that he be embalmed. Coroners were convinced there was no foul play and ordered the body returned to the artist's estate; the executor can decide whether to cremate, store, or publicly display it.

UNINTENDED CONSEQUENCES

When events

unexpectedly take on

a life of their own.

WORLD HEALTH ORGANIZATION PROVES HARMFUL

Early 1950s: Faced with a malaria outbreak in Borneo, the World Health Organization decided the simple solution would be to spray DDT. The insecticide killed the mosquitoes, solving the malaria problem, but it also entered the food chain via DDT-laden insects, which were eaten by geckos, which were eaten by cats—all of which died. With the cats gone, the rat population exploded, spreading plague and typhus. New cats had to be parachuted in to save the area from catastrophe.

In a parallel series of events, the DDT killed wasps that fed on thatch-eating caterpillars, which were now free to eat, unchecked, the thatched roofs common throughout Borneo, causing them to fall in on people's heads.

CRASH VICTIM ITCHES TO BE RESCUED

1941: When good Samaritans in Mexico, Missouri, spied a man in a car wreck, they rushed to his aid. They carefully extracted him from the wreck and gently laid him in a bed of poison ivy.

CONSTITUENTS VOTE WITH THEIR STOMACHS

January 1950: Victor Biaka-Boda represented his native Ivory Coast in the French senate. While on tour in his home country, the former witch doctor wanted to prove to voters that he was a caring representative who was truly at their disposal. In one of the more remote parts of his constituency he encountered a tribe of cannibals—who, upon seeing that he was sincerely concerned with their welfare and survival, ate him for supper.

JOKER'S FREEDOM CONSTRICTED AFTER BOA PRANK

2003: A pet-shop owner and practical joker in Innsbruck, Austria, did not have the last laugh when his latest prank backfired. Having once left a tarantula on the bar of his friend's restaurant, this time he thought it would be fun to sneak up behind the same friend and drape a huge boa constrictor over his shoulders. The snake immediately bit the restaurateur in front of his horrified customers. The friend was treated at a local hospital. The prankster was treated at the local police station.

MAN WINS LOTTERY, LOSES EVERYTHING

February 1988: A man who won $16 million in the Pennsylvania lottery lived to regret it. His girlfriend and family, determined to separate him from his newfound wealth, borrowed money that they never returned, convinced him to invest in shady businesses, sued him for winnings they believed they were entitled to, and as a last resort, hired a hit man to speed up their inheritance. By the time lawyers and the IRS cleaned up the mess, the man was cleaned out.

Silver lining: The winner is now leading a peaceful, happy life—poorer, but mercifully left alone.

CROW SETS OFF CHAIN OF DOOM

1942: It's like a page from one of Rube Goldberg's notebooks. A rancher in California shot at an annoying crow. The blast frightened the man's horse, whose shod hooves struck a rock, which sent sparks flying, which started a fire that burned 25 acres of land. The crow flew away unharmed.

MAN ARRANGES BIRTHDAY BLAST

2003: A Norwegian man, who found out about a surprise party being given for him, thought he'd surprise his guests by hiding in the woods near the party and shooting off his shotgun. When the celebrants arrived, he jumped out of his hiding place and tripped, blasting his friends with a round that sent six of them to the hospital.

ET TU, FARTUS?

2003: To give visitors a realistic trip back in time, the Dewa Roman Experience in Chester, England, re-creates the sights, sounds, and even smells of ancient Roman Britain. The 2003 latrine exhibit was a little too successful—schoolchildren became sick after smelling simulated Roman flatulence. The aroma makers promised to reformulate the farts to be less offensive.

SOMETIMES THE SKY REALLY IS FALLING . . .

IT'S RAINING— TVS!

2003: In five separate incidents, Romanian soccer fans—who all became infuriated when a Swiss referee gave Denmark the victory at the end of a tied game, thus eliminating the Romanian team from the 2004 European championships—ripped the cables from the walls and chucked their televisions out the windows.

MINKS COAT ENGLISH COUNTRYSIDE

1998: Members of the Animal Liberation Front broke into a mink farm in Hampshire, England, and released 6,000 minks. Although bred in captivity, minks are ferocious predators. They immediately fanned out into the countryside and began attacking cats, dogs, small farm animals, and an owl sanctuary. Officials feared they would enter houses through pet doors and wreak havoc within.

Adding insult to injury: Despite the intention of the ALF to give the minks a better life, most of the escapees would ultimately die of starvation.

BAD SPORTS

When the

competition gets

really ugly

RACE CAR CARNAGE REKINDLES OLD HATRED

June 11, 1955: Near the start of the annual LeMans auto race in France, Mercedes driver Pierre Levegh lost control of his car and plowed into a retaining wall, killing himself and 80-some spectators and injuring many others in the crowded stands. Despite the carnage, LeMans officials declined to call off the race because they feared that a mass exodus of spectators would block the roads and impede ambulance travel. Appalled by what they took to be callousness on the part of the race organizers, 80 percent of the spectators left and the Germans withdrew their entries, prompting the French to publicly remind them of what they did in the war. A long and ugly debate followed in the international press.

BELITTLING OCCUPATION OUTLAWED

2002: A three-foot ten-inch French dwarf may now face poverty—but with his dignity intact. In 1999, France banned dwarf-throwing, a bar sport imported from the United States and Australia in which a dwarf wearing a helmet and protective gear is flung as far as possible across the room. The tiny French stuntman brought a suit before the United Nations, claiming that the French ban was discriminatory, but the Human Rights Commission did not rule in his favor.

HAIRY ASSES FIGHT OVER WHOSE ASS IS HAIRIER

2002: An argument between two New Jersey friends over whose buttocks were hairier got out of hand when one man drew a knife and slashed the other's head. The injured party was taken to the hospital, his friend to the police station.

WEST GERMAN BUSINESSMAN SLICES AND DICES COUNTRYMEN

2002: A couple from the former East Germany bought a plastic vegetable slicer while on vacation at a spa in the former West Germany. When they got home, they decided they didn't like it and returned it to the vendor by mail. He sent them a refund—and also included a diatribe that blamed them and all East Germans for Germany's economic woes since the unification, claiming that many businessmen in the west would pay to rebuild the Berlin Wall, "preferably twice as high." The German press had a field day with the scandal. The vendor and the mayor of his Bavarian town apologized to the couple and to all East Germans.

I TOLD YOU SO!

A gallery of

unfortunate souls

who thought they

knew better . . .

but didn't

SWEATY MAN INSTANTLY REGRETS COOLING DIP

2000: In spite of warnings to stay out of a crocodile-infested river in Borneo, a British man—hot and sweaty from a day of exploring the rain forest—decided he couldn't resist a dip in the water. A crocodile decided he couldn't resist having a snack and instantly ate him.

TORTOISE TROUNCES TRAGEDIAN

456 B.C.: Aeschylus, the father of ancient Greek tragedy, fearlessly went out walking every day, despite an oracle's prediction that he would be killed by a blow from heaven. While living in retirement in Sicily, he went for his daily constitutional and was struck in the head and killed by a

tortoise that fell from the sky. An eagle had captured the hapless reptile and carried it aloft, then apparently mistook the playwright's bald pate for a rock on which to crack it open.

REVELERS REVEALED TO BE RESISTANT TO COMMON SENSE

August 10, 1856: Despite stormy weather and a hurricane forecast, a grand ball scheduled at the Trade Wind Hotel on Isle Derniere, a sand spit off the Louisiana coast, was held anyway. Several hundred revelers crowded the ballroom and partied on into the night, oblivious of the hurricane-force winds and waves outside. Just before midnight, the raging sea swallowed up the hotel, sweeping most of the people inside it to their deaths.

MILITARY ROCKS THE BOAT

September 1880: Insubordination and panic created a disaster during what were to be routine military maneuvers on the Ebro River in Spain. Almost 300 officers and recent recruits to the Spanish infantry were transported across the river on a pontoon raft while a military band played march music. Despite orders to cease stomping along with the music, the recruits continued to do so. When the raft began to seriously list, the troops panicked and managed to capsize it, throwing them all into the raging river.

KING CROESUS MISUNDERSTANDS ORACLE

ca. 546 B.C.: Unhappy being merely the wealthiest and most powerful king in Asia Minor, King Croesus of Lydia was obsessed with conquering the Persian Empire. When he consulted the Oracle at Delphi about his expansionist plans, the Sibyl replied, "You will destroy a great empire." Not bothering to ask which empire, Croesus thought he'd found the answer he was looking for and attacked Persia in about 546 B.C. King Cyrus of Persia not only destroyed Croesus's army but conquered Lydia as well.

THEATER OF DEATH

Long ago, people

found ways to entertain

themselves that give new

meaning to "hanging out"

and "killing time."

CRIMINALS IN HOT WATER

1530: Always in search of new and creative ways to dispatch convicted criminals (and please the crowd who came to watch), executioners at Smithfield Prison in London decided that poisoners should be boiled alive. A man named Roose, a cook who poisoned his master, was placed in a cauldron of cold water and slung over a roaring fire—where he took two hours to die. The executioners, thinking a little more clemency was in order, resolved that the liquid should already be boiling when the next prisoner was thrown in.

ADVICE TO LONDON BRIDGE PEDESTRIANS:
HEADS UP!

1305: The tradition of leaving traitors' heads to rot on London Bridge originated with the execution of Scottish nationalist William Wallace. For the next 350 years, traitors' heads were impaled next to Drawbridge Gate, the official entrance to London, as a warning to all. In  politically tough times, dozens of heads were on display, prompting the official Keeper of the Heads to dump the old ones in the river to make room for the new.

SEE YOU IN HELL . . .

July 21, 1683: "I hope I shall soon see a much better assembly!" So said William, Lord Russell, upon mounting the scaffold and surveying the bloodthirsty throng gathered to see him lose his head for taking part in an attempted assassination of King Charles II of England. Not only was Russell wrongly convicted, as was later discovered, but the executioner was having a bad day and needed three strikes of the ax to finish Russell off.

NOOSE SURVIVOR'S NEXT SENTENCE: AMERICA

1740: After 16-year-old rapist-murderer William Duell was hanged for his crimes, his body was cut down and taken to Surgeon's Hall in London for medical dissection. While cleaning the "corpse," a servant noticed it was still breathing. Within a couple of hours, Duell had completely revived and was dispatched to Newgate Prison. At the next session of the Old Bailey (the criminal court in London), the judges gave him a different sort of death sentence—transport to the American colonies.

SOMETIMES THE SKY REALLY IS FALLING . . .

IT'S RAINING— REALLY BIG HAIL!

May 8, 1784: Hailstones almost nine inches in circumference fell in colonial Winnsboro, South Carolina, killing several men and many birds, cattle, and horses in the pasturelands. It was the only fatal hail shower to occur in the United States until 1979, when hail killed a baby in Fort Collins, Colorado. The largest officially documented hailstone to fall in the United States—in Coffeyville, Kansas, on September 3, 1970— was 5.67 inches across and weighed 1.67 pounds.

CITIZENS PREVENTED FROM HANGING OUT ALONG ROUTE TO GALLOWS

1783: The "theater of the scaffold"—aka public hangings—always drew a sellout crowd, but by 1783 the mob in London had grown so rowdy that magistrates, fearing an insurrection, banned the procession of convicts from Newgate Prison to the hanging place on Tyburn Hill. Instead of seeing the condemned and their crimes as a moral lesson in piety, the crowd often treated them as heroes, cheering them on and offering them drinks and mocking the law. Public hangings continued, but the jeering, unruly crowd was now confined to the smaller, more controllable area around the scaffold.

LOVE AND MARRIAGE

*Many a good hanging
prevents a bad marriage.*
—WILLIAM SHAKESPEARE, *The Tempest*

PREMARITAL COUNSELING?

2002: In Serbia, husbands-to-be can now determine ahead of time whether their future wives are witches. The test is held at Djundjerski Castle in Kulpin, where the woman is weighed standing and again when she's seated on a broomstick. To show she's not a witch, she must weigh more the second time, proving that the broomstick is not supporting her weight. The test began as a tourist attraction for the castle, but a growing number of nervous grooms are taking it seriously.

Love, Romanian Style

In the good old days, you had to have really good, Ten Commandments–grade grounds to get a divorce. In 21st-century Romania, seemingly anything goes:

- In 2001, a Romanian woman divorced her husband because she was jealous that he was thin, claiming he was taunting her with his constant trips to the kitchen to pig out.

- That same year, a man was almost laughed out of court when he told the judge he wanted a divorce because his wife wouldn't stop cooking with so much garlic.

- In 2002, another man decided he'd had enough and ended their 30-year marriage when his wife forgot to make him lamb for Easter.

- And in 2003, a woman demanded a divorce after her husband kept calling out the name of his first wife while he slept. His current wife claimed he was cheating on her in his dreams.

MARRIAGE RENDERED MOOT—OR MEAT

1897: When Louisa Bicknese Luetgert disappeared from her Chicago home on May 1, her relatives, who knew of her troubled marriage, immediately suspected her husband. Detectives ultimately found her wedding ring at the bottom of one of the rendering vats in her husband's sausage factory. Adolf Luetgert was convicted of murder and sentenced to life in prison. He probably burned his wife's body, but rumors spread that he had ground her into links, although none of his customers had complained.

CRAZED HUSBAND DECONSTRUCTS ARCHITECT

June 25, 1906: Obsessed with the premarital affairs of his wife, Evelyn Nesbit, Harry Thaw shot and killed prominent architect Stanford White during a performance at the roof-

garden theater of Madison Square Garden. Thaw claimed White was a "beast" who had stolen his wife's virginity when she was only 16. Nesbit, who had been an artist's model and stage actress since coming to New York at 15, had dated several other prominent men, including actor John Barrymore, before she married Thaw, who was heir to more than $40 million. Stanford White's debauched lifestyle became the focus of the trial, and despite dozens of witnesses to the shooting, Thaw was found not guilty by reason of insanity. Reporters dubbed it the "crime of the century."

WILLIAM BURROUGHS PLAYS WILLIAM TELL

September 1951: After many years with the paranoid, heroin-addicted, and generally deranged writer William Burroughs, his wife, Joan, agreed to a game of William Tell. Using a revolver instead of a bow and arrow, Burroughs attempted to shoot a glass of water off his wife's head. Unfortunately for Joan, he missed the glass, and she died instantly. Fortunately for Burroughs, the incident took place in Mexico, where his attorneys convinced the judge that it was all an accident. Burroughs fled to Europe before Mexican authorities could deport him to the United States.

LOVE THY NEIGHBOR

Now you'll understand why the Bible commands us thus. The alternative can be most unpleasant.

WOULD-BE SUPERMAN SUPS ON NEIGHBOR

2003: Believing that eating human flesh would give him supernatural powers, an Indonesian man dug up his freshly deceased neighbor, took the corpse home, and was still working his way through it when police arrested him days later. Found sane by the court, he was sentenced to five years' imprisonment for grave robbing and cannibalism.

SENIORITY RULES IN BORDER DISPUTE

2003: Two feisty German women, with a combined age of 172, got into a row over a fence separating their properties. The fight ended with the elder one, a 95-year-old grandmother, hitting her (relatively) younger neighbor over the head with a garden spade. The latter was treated for cuts and bruises; the more senior senior citizen faced assault charges.

DRUG COUNSELOR POWERLESS TO HELP HOPPED-UP NEIGHBOR

2002: A former drug-and-alcohol-abuse counselor in Denver, Colorado, was nearly made homeless when her neighbor's house exploded. The neighbor had been  cooking up methamphetamines in his kitchen when his home lab burst into flames, driving him out of the house and into the arms of police. It was the fourth such incident in Denver in less than four weeks. The drug counselor's power was temporarily knocked out, but her house was left standing.

HATFIELD V. MCCOY

1864–1890: The bad blood between the Hatfields and the McCoys, two Appalachian farming families living on either side of the West Virginia–  Kentucky border, dated back to the Civil War, when a Confederacy-sympathizing Hatfield killed a McCoy who'd served in the Union army. Tensions simmered until 1878 when Randall McCoy, having accused Floyd Hatfield of stealing his pigs, didn't find satisfaction in court and took matters into his own hands. A Romeo and Juliet romance between the families only escalated the hostilities. Finally, in the late 1880s, the Kentucky McCoys appealed to the state to bring the West Virginia Hatfields to justice— but not before there were more killings on both sides. Finally, in 1890, Ellison Mount, a Hatfield cousin, went to the gallows for murder and another half-dozen Hatfields served time in prison. By the mid-1890s, the feud had spent itself.

OUT OF TOUCH

Getting lost in

time and space

PROFESSOR'S ACADEMIC CAREER CRAWLS TO A HALT

1925: In London, a biology professor noticed an interesting snail crawling along the railroad tracks. To observe its habits, he crawled after it and became so engrossed that he didn't notice the train behind him. Both professor and snail were dispatched to oblivion.

JAPANESE SOLDIER MISSES END OF WAR BY 30 YEARS

March 9, 1974: In December 1944, Lieutenant Hiroo Onoda was stationed with a small band of soldiers on a remote island in the Philippines and ordered to wage guerilla war against the enemy until instructed otherwise by his army superiors. Japan surrendered the following autumn, but not Onoda, even after his soldiers ran away and various contingents of friends, relatives, and envoys from the Japanese government tried to convince him that the war was over. Onoda believed that the Japanese would commit suicide before surrendering and that all these people were enemy imposters. Finally someone found one of Onoda's former superior officers, took him to the island, and had him order the holdout to lay down his sword. Onoda finally surrendered in March 1974, 30 years after he began his fight.

ECCENTRIC BROTHERS EXCAVATED BY POLICE

March 21, 1947: The Collyer brothers, Homer and Langley, started their lives as the privileged sons of a wealthy New York physician. By the time police were called to their Fifth Avenue brownstone and found them dead inside, they had been recluses for years, living without electricity or running water, having amassed a collection of junk and newspapers that was packed floor to ceiling in every room. Homer, blind since 1933 and dependent on his brother, had starved to death because Langley had been crushed by his own booby trap, which he rigged up to drop piles of newspapers on any intruder. It took three weeks of digging through the house for police to find Langley's body.

CAUGHT WITH YOUR PANTS DOWN

Best to keep your belt buckled and wear clean underwear, like your mother told you.

POLICE PURSUE FLAMING PANTS

2002: When police in Tallahassee, Florida, attempted to arrest a man for urinating in public one night, he pulled up his pants and ran. Chasing him was easy because the lit cigarette he'd parked in his pants while doing his business had ignited the garment. The suspect finally lost his grip on the fiery britches, which slipped down and tripped him. The police put out the fire, then hauled him off to the station to cool down.

COPS BUST COWORKER FOR WIFE'S BUST

2001: In what she thought would be a private affair, a policeman's wife posted nude pictures of herself on the Web to surprise and delight her husband. Unfortunately, his superiors came across the photos on the police department's computer system and were so surprised that they suspended the officer for three days without pay.

COUPLE TOO SELF-AMUSING AT AMUSEMENT PARK

2000: After enjoying their day at King's Island, a family amusement park in Ohio, a couple repaired to a photo booth to enjoy and document a favorite erotic act. Unfortunately, they did not realize that a monitor on the outside of the booth broadcast the goings-on to passersby.

By the time park employees caught on, a crowd had gathered to watch. The employees desperately tried to cover the monitor while security guards broke up the act inside the booth.

CRIMINAL DUTCHMAN TREATS SELF IN TOURIST'S NETHER LAND

2003: A man doing his business in a gas station men's room stall in Holland was shocked to see a hand come under the partition to snatch his wallet and car keys. By the time he pulled up his pants and got to the parking lot, his car was missing and his wallet was on the ground, with the cash gone.

MAN HANGS OUT, GETS FIXED

2003: A Croatian flasher spotted a woman in her garden, dropped his pants, and pushed his private parts through a hole in her fence. The woman's dog immediately bit him. Doctors treating him at a local hospital turned him over to police when they found out how he was injured.

IT'S IN THEIR NATURE

When instinct

runs amok

GATOR ARMED TO THE TEETH

2002: The director of the Kanapaha Botanical Gardens in Gainesville, Florida, lost his arm in a surprise attack by a resident alligator while weeding an area near a water-lily pond. He happened to brush up against the gator, which swallowed his arm whole after chomping it off below the elbow. Authorities killed the gator, slit open its stomach, and found the severed arm, but doctors were unable to reattach it.

MAN BITES DOG

2003: A drunken man bit a German shepherd police dog on the neck while resisting arrest during an altercation outside a Syracuse, New York, bar. By the time a policeman got him to release the dog, the assailant had two black eyes and a broken nose. The dog was sore from the bite, but at least he got a couple of sick days out of it.

AUSSIE DEVELOPS TASTE FOR YANK SHEILA

1987: The Land Down Under is home to koalas, kangaroos, and fearless, sneaky, 15-foot saltwater crocodiles that not only kill and maim in the usual ways, but can also jump out of the water and attack people in boats. One such cunning croc made a snack of an attractive American model when she and a friend went swimming in Prince Regent River in 1987. When the crocodile sidled up beside them, the girls swam to a nearby ledge and tried to scare it away by throwing things at it. The monster didn't budge, and when the model tried to swim around it to safety, it devoured her.

A FRIEND IN NEED IS A MEAL INDEED

1824: Eight vicious criminals escaped from an Australian prison and wandered deep into the bush to elude capture. Before long they were starving, and within a few weeks only Alexander Pierce remained; he had eaten all seven of his comrades. When the British captured him, they thought he was lying to cover up for the other escapees. But after returning to prison, he ate a fellow convict, and the authorities had him executed. His skull was shipped to America, where it was analyzed by phrenologists and is still on display in the Philadelphia Academy of Natural Sciences.

DOG BITES SHARKS

2003: A wild dog that wandered into the town hall in Cuttack, India, went on a biting spree that left eight lawyers smarting. The hall, which housed the courts, was overrun by dogs and other animals, including fierce, wild bulls that frequented the building and the surrounding veranda. The local bar association complained that building officials have ignored court orders to clear the building.

Animal Court Is Now in Session

From the Middle Ages to the early 20th century, animals were tried and sentenced for their crimes, not because they were deemed dangerous, but because the Church believed they were intelligent and therefore responsible for their actions.

- In 1451, a bunch of leeches in Lausanne (in what is now Switzerland) bought themselves an exorcism when they "refused" to leave town.

- In 1457, a French sow was hanged for killing and eating a small child. Her brood, which were tried with her, were pardoned because of their age.

- In 1474, in Basle, Switzerland, a cock was burned at the stake as a sorcerer. The townsfolk believed he was possessed by the devil after he laid an egg without a yolk.

- In 1713, Franciscan friars in Brazil demanded that the Church excommunicate the termites that were consuming their monastery. At the ecclesiastical trial the termites' defense argued successfully that they had been there first. The bugs were allotted their own piece of land to eat at will.

- In 1916, in Erwin, Tennessee, "Five-Ton Mary," an elephant in the menagerie of Sparks Circus, killed one of her trainers and was executed, by hanging, the following day.

SWORDFISH PREPARES MAN-KEBOB

2000: A Mexican man deep-sea fishing off the coast near Acapulco got a nasty surprise when the ten-foot marlin he was reeling in suddenly jumped out of the water and into his boat, piercing him straight through the abdomen with its spear. The fisherman was alive after the attack but unable to get up or signal for help. A passing vessel rescued him two days later and took him to a hospital.

WHEN ANIMALS ARE WEAPONS

Have an urge to go

on a robbing spree and

can't find your gun?

Have you ever thought of

packing a snake?

SMARMY THIEF MAKES SWARMY GETAWAY

MEN

2003: A shoplifter at a K-Mart in Sedalia, Missouri, got away with his loot by releasing a swarm of bees. Suspecting he was up to no good, security guards followed the man to the restroom. When they opened the door, they were confronted with about 100 honeybees. The shoplifter slipped away while employees pulled cans of insecticide off the shelves to kill the buzzers.

APES AND SNAKES THREATEN PARISIAN SHOPPERS

2000: In a scene straight out of "The Murders in the Rue Morgue," thieves in Paris used live Barbary apes and venomous snakes to mug people in the streets and on the Metro. Instead of being shot or stabbed, horrified victims were threatened with mauling and biting if they didn't hand over their valuables.

Nature (and the black market) abhors a vacuum: A crackdown on pit bulls in and around Paris increased the illegal importation of Barbary apes into France.

Vigilante Animal-Justice

Even though some animals have become unwitting pawns in the hands of criminals, others have done all they could to thwart criminals where they found them:

- In 2002, an accused murderer was sent up the river for good when a civic-minded crocodile caught him trying to jump the border and ate him for supper. The consumed criminal, who was awaiting trial for killing a judge, had escaped from his jail cell and was attempting to cross the jungle from Costa Rica to his native Panama.

- The following year, a dog in Germany refused to leave a butcher's establishment with his master, who was robbing the place. The burglar had given the dog a pack of sausages to keep it busy while he cleaned the place out. The dog's hoarding of the meaty treasure delayed the man's escape long enough for police to arrive and arrest him.

- In 2006, a macaw savagely attacked a burglar who had broken into his home while his owners were away. The marks the bird left on the man made him easy to identify by police, who got a quick confession out of him when confronted with evidence of the avian brawl.

UNDERMINED FOUNDATIONS

The earth is mankind's ultimate haven, our blessed terra firma. When it trembles and gives way beneath our feet, it's as though one of God's cheques has bounced.

—GILBERT ADAIR

BEAUVAIS CATHEDRAL COLLAPSES

1284: Saint-Pierre de Beauvais Cathedral boasted the tallest vaulted gothic space in France until the roof collapsed one Friday night. A defective foundation, not enough

internal roof supports, and gale-force winds coming off the English Channel have all been blamed. The roof was rebuilt and work continued on the cathedral for generations. By 1569, the spire soared over 500 feet. In 1573, it collapsed again.

Beginning of the end: The same structural problems continue to plague Beauvais. It is now on the World Monuments Watch of the 100 Most Endangered Sites.

OLD MAN LOSES FACE

2003: After 30,000 years of gazing over the Franconia Notch State Park region of New Hampshire's White Mountains, the rock face known as the Old Man of the Mountain collapsed after a night of thawing and refreezing. The granite outcropping had been unstable for years, and attempts to hold it in place with cables, spikes, and glue proved no match for the forces of gravity. Although the Old Man still appears on the New Hampshire quarter, his disappearance could mean a downturn in tourism for the area. Franconia's town moderator, David Schaffer, suggested that the town might put up signs reading See Where the Old Man Was but conceded, "We'd only be able to get away with that for about a year."

TOWER OF PISA ON COUNTDOWN TO COLLAPSE

1174: The Leaning Tower of Pisa has been a disaster since the first stone was laid. It was meant to surpass every other tower in Italy in height and beauty, but it began to sink into the ground before the first story was finished. The additional stories were designed to compensate for the lean—the bell tower at the top, completed in 1350, was constructed at an angle to the rest of the building in order to appear straight, but it, too, now leans. Modern technology has shored up the tower's foundation but cannot stop the settling, which proceeds at the rate of a half inch per year. Unless something else can be done, the tower will collapse within the next two centuries.

MULHOLLAND'S DAM COLLAPSES

March 13, 1928: Eager to supply more water for an ever-thirsty Los Angeles, in 1926 William Mulholland oversaw the building of the Saint Francis Dam. However, the modern, 175-foot-high dam was built on a rocky foundation that lay over a fault zone. Two years later the earth shifted and, just minutes before midnight on March 12, the dam gave way. The impounded waters of the old Santa Clara River swiftly rolled to the sea, sweeping away everything in their path, including approximately 450 people living in the Santa Clara Valley.

ROOF FALLS, JUST MISSING ARCHITECTS

1979: After a drenching thunderstorm overwhelmed the drainage system on the roof of the Crosby Kemper Memorial Arena in Kansas City, Missouri, the building collapsed. Fortunately, the building was empty, and there were no injuries. Ironically, the American Institute of Architects, who had given the arena's architects an award for design excellence in 1976, were in the arena the day before for their annual convention.

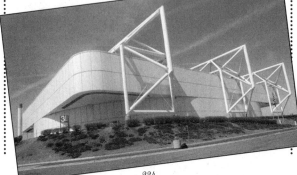

STADIUM CRUSHES ANCIENT ROMANS

A.D. 27: The huge wooden amphitheater at Fidenae, in a suburb of ancient Rome, suddenly collapsed right before a gladiatorial contest was to begin. More than 50,000 spectators had crowded into the brand-new stadium in anticipation of the bloody event, only to meet death themselves under crashing timbers, heavy rubble, and a shower of bodies that cascaded from the collapsing stands to the bottom of the arena floor.

Some things never change: Corrupt contractors and shoddy construction practice were to blame. The builders cut corners in laying the foundation, which shifted under the massive weight of the crowd, causing the stadium itself to collapse.

BON APPÉTIT

You don't want

to know

what goes on

in some kitchens.

FOOD FOR THOUGHT

2003: Surgeons in China figured out what was causing one man's mental disorder—a four-inch-long worm that was living inside his brain. The doctors were unsure how the parasite got into his head and speculated that the man's regular consumption of frogs and snakes might have been the source of his problem.

THE HAND THAT ROCKS THE LADLE

2003: Every diner's worst nightmare was realized when a mass outbreak of salmonella poisoning at an Austrian restaurant was attributed by health-department officials to employees' not washing their hands after using the toilet. The restaurant owner subsequently installed closed-circuit cameras in the bathrooms to monitor his staff's hygiene.

FAST FOOD THAT'LL MAKE YOU WANT TO FAST

2002: A young man made an unexpected trip to the emergency room in Lexington, Tennessee, after biting into a burger and discovering that the meat was bat. The teenage cook at the fast-food joint where the "burger" originated found the dead bat, which had been run over by a car, and thought it would be a great prank to put it on a bun and serve it. The joke was now on her—she faced criminal charges. The bat tested negative for rabies.

CABIN BOY'S FANTASTIC VOYAGE

July 3, 1884: During a four-day storm off the coast of West Africa, a freak 40-foot wave sank the *Mignonette,* a sailing yacht being transported from England to Australia. The four-man crew took refuge in a small dinghy. After almost two weeks of blistering sun, thirst, and hunger, the other three ate the cabin boy. Because they had not followed the "custom of the sea" and drawn lots to select their victim, the captain and one crewmate were convicted of murder (the other mate testified against them). They were pardoned six months later.

Shortly after the trial, Madame Tussauds Chamber of Horrors displayed a waxwork of "The Cannibal Captain, Tom Dudley."

PARISIANS EMPTY ZOO ONTO THEIR PLATES

1870-71: The Franco-Prussian War created such food shortages in France that Parisians were regularly forced to eat dogs, cats, and rats to supplement their diet. Newspapers even published recipes that reflected the new circumstance, including one for "Gigot de chien flanque de ratons"—dog leg with rat flank. By the end of 1870, the Paris Zoo, unable to feed its animals, was forced to turn them over to local butchers. Buffalo, zebra, and even elephant ended up on plates all over Paris. Only the lions and tigers were spared, as they were judged too dangerous to slaughter.

CHEF GIVES CUSTOMERS A HEADS-UP

2002: A disgruntled former employee of a restaurant in Quito, Ecuador, brought the health department down on his boss's head for using human skull fragments in his cooking. The cook didn't deny the charge—the way other chefs use truffles to impart extra flavor, he used skull shavings to give his customers good luck. Not surprisingly, the health commissioner deemed the ingredient a danger to public health and ordered the restaurant closed.

SOMETIMES THE SKY REALLY IS FALLING . . .

IT'S RAINING— SPACECRAFT!

Two years after its launch in May 1960, a 21-pound chunk of the USSR spaceship *Sputnik* IV crashed onto a Wisconsin street, burrowing several inches into the ground. Almost 20 years later, the U.S. Space Station *Skylab* began to break up and fall to Earth over the Southern Hemisphere. The largest piece to hit land was a one-ton tank. Luckily the debris did not cause any damage or fatalities when it crashed to Earth.

THE WEATHER CHANNEL

You don't need to pray to God anymore when there are storms in the sky, but you do have to be insured.

—Bertolt Brecht

WETTEST DAY SINCE NOAH

1952: Réunion island wasn't a good place to be on March 15 and 16. That's when 73.62 inches of rain fell on the island just east of Madagascar, making it the wettest 24 hours on record. The record-breaking rain came in the middle of a three-day rainstorm that dumped almost 100 inches (more than eight feet) of rain.

THE BLIZZARD OF 1888

March 11, 1888: The forecast called for "light snow, then clearing," but a three-day blizzard overwhelmed the eastern seaboard, dumping two to four feet of snow in parts of Pennsylvania, New Jersey, New York, and New England. Temperatures plummeted, 80-mile-per-hour winds piled snow into 15- to 20-foot drifts, telegraph poles snapped, and trains and streetcars derailed, paralyzing the region for days.

RAIN REIGNS A LITTLE TOO SUPREME

1950: A prolonged water shortage in New York City prompted officials to call in a rainmaker to seed the clouds above the city's reservoirs in the Catskill region. Little happened over the summer, except for protests by Catskill-area businessmen

SOMETIMES THE SKY REALLY IS FALLING . . .

IT'S RAINING— ROOFS!

2003: After a nasty storm in Germany, a distraught woman called police to arrest the owners of a wayward roof that landed on her Volkswagen Golf. Pressing charges was not an option, but the woman was still determined to find the responsible party through public appeals and a house-to-house search for a home that was missing a roof.

who claimed the threat of rain would destroy their tourist season. In late November, hunters in the Catskills said they saw the clouds being seeded again, and a few days later a torrential downpour struck the area, damaging property in three upstate counties. New York's water shortage was at an end, but the lawsuits were just beginning.

THE GREAT TORNADO OF 1925

March 18, 1925: A powerful tornado cut a swath of destruction through five states. The twister originated in California, then raged across Colorado and south into Missouri, before spending its final fury in Indiana and Illinois. Sympathy and aid poured into the region, as did 100,000 midwestern tourists to gawk at hardest-hit Princeton, Indiana. The National Guard kept watch over the huge crowds who turned the ravaged landscape into picnic grounds.

SUDDENLY LOST SUMMER

April 5, 1815: Twelve thousand people in Java had the worst day of their soon-to-be-ended lives when Mount Tambora erupted with such force that 30 cubic miles of dust were  thrown into the atmosphere, affecting worldwide weather for years. The following year, summer bypassed the Northern Hemisphere. There were blizzards in Connecticut in June; temperatures in the northern United States did not budge beyond the 50-degree mark during daytime and fell below freezing at night. The freak season caused crop failures throughout Europe and sparked the great German migration to America in the 1820s.

TEMPESTUOUS GLORIA DRIVES TRUCKER TO DRINK

September 1985: When Hurricane Gloria hit the eastern seaboard, a truck driver went for the ride of his life when the storm's 100-mile-an-hour winds blew his vehicle off the Verrazano Narrows Bridge in New York City. Although the truck fell 90 feet into the Hudson River, the lucky driver survived.

TORNADO HITS TOWN, SWEEPS UP AFTER ITSELF

March 16, 1942: Although the paths of tornadoes can be difficult to predict, they often hit the same places again and again. The town of Baldwyn, Mississippi, was unlucky enough to be hit by two tornadoes only 25 minutes apart. Most of the 65 fatalities occurred when people emerged from their shelters after the first tornado, unaware that the second was upon them.

TRANSYLVANIA STATION

Just what you would

expect—vampires,

crypts, and

all things Dracula

VAMPIROPHOBE SLAYS SELF WITH GARLIC CLOVE

January 1973: Despite living and working in England for more than 25 years, a Polish immigrant never lost his old-country fear of vampires. He surrounded himself with objects designed to keep vampires away, dusted his bed nightly with salt (a lesser-known deterrent), stuffed garlic in keyholes, and even slept with a clove of garlic in his mouth. The latter proved to be his undoing. When he had not been seen for a number of days, his landlady called the police, who broke down his door and discovered that he had choked on a clove of garlic.

DRACULA COUNTESS DISCOVERS FOUNTAIN OF YOUTH

1600s: The local virgins of Transylvania had no idea what they were in for when their parents enrolled them in a "finishing school" for the daughters of aristocrats, run by the Countess Erzsébet Báthori (Elizabeth Bathory) of Transylvania. Obsessed with remaining youthful, she tried many cures for aging before discovering that a daily bath in virgin's blood did the trick. She went through numerous local peasant girls before opening her "finishing school" to ensure a fresh supply of virgins. By the time her gruesome secret was discovered in 1611, almost 700 young girls had been sacrificed to the countess's vanity.

CREEPY CRYPT FOUND IN FAMILY HOME

2002: A Romanian family living in Sibui, Transylvania, discovered that the house they'd live in for over 50 years had a gruesome secret when a plumber dug into the cellar floor to repair a pipe. The floor concealed more than 2,000 skeletons, which dated back to the 14th century. They had probably been dumped at the site when a local cemetery was moved to make way for a cathedral in the 1400s. Although local authorities arranged to have the skeletons removed and reinterred in a local cemetery, the family made no bones about not returning to the house.

Down for the Count

1450s: Vlad V, ruler of Wallachia in Transylvania in the 15th century and the inspiration for Bram Stoker's Dracula, had such a fearsome reputation that it was usually enough to keep his enemies at bay:

- When some of his nobles offended him, he had them beheaded, fed the heads to crabs, and then served the crabs to the nobles' relatives.

- When a delegation of Turks refused to remove their turbans in his presence, Vlad had the headwear nailed to their heads.

- After a typical mass impaling, when one of his knights complained that the smell of death nauseated him, Vlad had him impaled, saying his soldiers must be able to stomach death. Vlad then had him raised higher than the rest of his victims, so he would not have to smell them.

- After giving a banquet for hundreds of local poor in his castle, Vlad and his henchmen slipped away and set the dining hall on fire, trapping the peasants inside. He claimed he was being merciful by freeing them from their wretched lives while they still had a full stomach.

HITCHING A RIDE

Sometimes we all need a lift.

FREQUENT FLY-ER MILES

2002: An English man who'd traveled through the South African rain forest didn't realize he'd brought back a nasty souvenir—the larva of a botfly. He'd been stung during the trip and, three months later, noticed the head of a live worm sticking out of what he'd thought was a simple mosquito bite. Doctors assured him that it was a common enough occurrence.

A species of human botfly attaches its eggs to a blood-sucking mosquito that it captures and then releases. When the mosquito comes in contact with humans or other warm-blooded animals, the fly eggs hatch and the larvae fasten to the mammal's skin. The larvae bore into muscle tissue; the infestation is called myiasis.

TWO THUMBS DOWN

1941: Two men outside Barcelona, Spain, hitched a ride on a truck carrying a casket, but when the coffin's lid popped open and what they thought was a dead man spoke  to them, they both leaped off the truck. One of the hitchhikers was killed, the other injured. The undead man had also hitched a ride on the truck and took refuge in the empty coffin when it started to rain.

GORILLA GONE WILD

2003: A 300-pound gorilla, determined to avail himself of the delights of Boston, twice escaped from the Franklin Park Zoo. The first time, he was caught outside the Tropical Forest Exhibit on his way to the exit. The second time, he injured two people as he made his way through the gates. He was spotted sitting at a bus stop, presumably on his way to a new life, and was apprehended later that day.

MAGGOT CARPET RIDE

July 1998: Health officials in Huntsville, Alabama, were alarmed when they learned that a local man who had recently returned from the Brazilian rain forest appeared to have brought back flesh-eating screwworms, which are capable of eating a large cow in less than a week. The man sought medical attention when he noticed sores on his scalp. Doctors believe screwworm flies laid maggots in a wound in his head while he was in the rain forest and the larvae fed  on his flesh until they hatched. Although the man was treated, authorities worried that if live maggots escaped from his house, they could infest the entire Huntsville area.

STOWAWAY SCORPION UNHAPPY ABOUT TRAVELING COACH

2002: After disembarking from his flight back from Hawaii, a Seattle man reached for his bag and got a nasty surprise—a sting on the hand by a scorpion that had hitched a ride in the luggage hold. In classic cockroach-killing fashion, another passenger immediately flattened it with his shoe. The man was treated at the local hospital and released.

SOMETIMES THE SKY REALLY IS FALLING . . .

IT'S RAINING—RECORD-BREAKING ROCKS!

March 8, 1976: A meteorite storm over China dumped more than 100 stones, many of them weighing 200 pounds or more, near the city of Jilin. The largest of the stones weighed 3,902 pounds.

GATORAMA

From endangered

to endangering—

gators gone wild

all over the world

GATOR GETS OFF ON TECHNICALITY

2000s: From 1967 to 1987, alligators were on the endangered-species list in Florida. During that time the alligators thrived—and so did humans, whose housing developments moved ever deeper into the Everglades region and other alligator habitats, making unhappy meetings of these two species inevitable. Florida officers received almost 17,000 alligator-complaint calls in 2001 alone, and the number was expected to grow. Currently there are about 1 million alligators and 17 million people trying to peacefully share the state of Florida.

In 2003, a Florida man spotted an alligator approaching a woman with four small children. He grabbed a rope, lassoed the gator, and called the police. Following the strict Florida laws governing gators, they made the man cut the rope, gave him a summons, and then called a trapper to catch the gator he had just freed.

ALLIGATOR CARJACKS FLORIDA MOTORIST

2002: A seven-foot alligator in Port Charlotte attacked a car on a local road, biting through the bumper and lifting it off the ground. The startled driver, thinking she had run over a small mammal, pulled the car over. After discovering what had her in its clutches, she put the car into reverse in order to escape. The gator was later tracked down and shot.

FLORIDA DEATH MATCH: GATORS 3, PYTHONS 1

2005: As if Floridians did not have enough problems with alligators wandering through their neighborhoods, a new species is now threatening their backyards:

Over the past 20 years, frightened owners of formerly cute little Burmese pythons have dumped hundreds of them into the Everglades, where they are now breeding 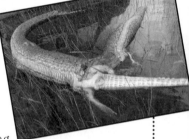 and competing with alligators for the role of top predator. Although the snakes, which can grow up to 20 feet long and weigh more than 200 pounds, are usually the losers in face-to-face battles, they seem to be gaining ground. In September 2005, park rangers found the carcasses of a 13-foot python that had swallowed a six-foot alligator, which, in its death throes, killed its attacker by bursting out of the python's gut.

AMPHIBIOUS IMMIGRANTS SEIZED IN SINGAPORE

2003: An advance team of nonnative crocodiles was rounded up in Singapore when members of the four-croc team were found checking out local transportation (a canal), housing (an apartment complex), recreation (a public park), and commercial interests (a bank). Authorities, who incarcerated them at the Singapore Zoo, still can't figure out how they got to the wealthy island nation or why they neglected to look into schools for their kids.

MINI-GODZILLA RUNS AMOK IN TOKYO

2002: A five-foot spectacled caiman—an alligator-like Central and South American crocodile—led police on a wild-reptile chase through a residential part of Tokyo. After passing hospitals, schools, parks, and many surprised pedestrians, it was finally lured into a dog cage.

Every year Japan imports hundreds of baby crocodilians, only inches in length, that are later abandoned.

Vanity of vanities: The alligator was first spotted loitering on the front steps of a beauty salon.

CROCS MOVE TO SUBURBS, SEEKING A BETTER LIFE

1998: Children in Westcourt, a heavily populated area in Queensland, Australia, often play on the banks of a storm drain that is fed by a creek. Six-foot

crocodiles also came to play one day, before environmental police apprehended and removed one from the area. Another had been spotted but scuttled back into the drain before officers could get to it.

Beginning of the end: Two months before, a 15-year-old girl had been grabbed and mauled by a croc in the same area. She escaped after her grandmother kicked the reptile in the head until it released her.

URBAN LEGEND LIVES!

2003: Queens, New York, residents taking in the spring sunshine in Alley Pond Park were surprised to find a real alligator basking along with them. Park rangers caught the three-foot sun worshipper and took it to the Bronx Zoo. They characterized it as one of many exotic pets that owners "abandon when they realize they're big enough to eat their child."

IF IT AIN'T BROKE . . .

New products that

produced only

bad results

NEW COKE?
TRY CLASSIC JOKE

1985: Sugar guzzlers across America were taken aback when, after 100 years of soft-drink success, the Coca-Cola Company changed its formula for Coke to make it taste more like Pepsi-Cola, which had been eating into Coke's market share. Panicked Coke lovers began hoarding the old soft drink. New Coke didn't last three months on the market before the old formula was reintroduced as Coke Classic. By 1993, New Coke had been forgotten and (old) Coke was once more the number one drink in America.

CARTER QUARTER WORTH PLUGGED NICKEL

1979–1980: In an effort to save $50-some million a year on printing paper money, the United States Mint decided to issue a one-dollar coin. Congress voted to put women's suffrage crusader Susan B. Anthony on the face of the coin, which had an 11-sided raised border to distinguish it from a quarter. It was issued in 1979 and 1980 and was a complete flop. Despite its multifaceted border, it was the same size and color as a quarter and caused confusion among merchants and consumers, who made the costly mistake, especially in the dark, of handing it over instead of a 25-cent piece. Dubbed the "Carter Quarter" because it was issued during Jimmy Carter's administration, which was marked by rampant inflation, it soon went the way of the two-dollar bill.

SMELL-O-VISION (STINK) BOMBS

1959–1960: The rise of television in the early 1950s caused a significant decline in movie

attendance. Desperate movie producers dreamed up dozens of schemes to lure audiences back, including systems designed to give a real sensory experience by allowing moviegoers to smell what was happening on the screen. "Aromarama" featured a scent track that pumped different scents through the air-conditioning system. "Smell-o-vision" delivered the scent directly to the movie seat by means of a tube. Both systems were resounding failures—not only because they were expensive and impractical but because they made audiences sick. Producers went back to the drawing board, seeking other gimmicks that did not stink more than the movies themselves.

THAT ACCURS'D SCOTTISH PLAY

From its very first performance in 1606, Shakespeare's *Macbeth* has been associated with disaster. During its premiere, the lad playing Lady Macbeth collapsed (and later died) and had to be replaced by Shakespeare himself. Later disasters include: a revival that opened on the day of the Great Storm of 1703, after which Queen Anne blamed the storm on the play and ordered all theaters closed for a week of prayers; rioting outside theaters where it was performed; injuries to cast members during rehearsals; and, of course, really bad reviews. Tradition holds that no actor may mention the play by name while in the theater—they should instead refer to it by one of its many euphemisms: "That Play," "The Comedy of Glamis," and "The Scottish Business."

DON QUIXOTE: *THE "SCOTTISH PLAY" OF CINEMA?*

Director Terry Gilliam worried that filming *Don Quixote* was a jinxed project: Orson Welles went broke with his unfinished version in the 1950s, and Gilliam feared his own film was turning into a $31 million sinkhole, thanks to cost overruns, bad weather, ailing actors, and other acts of God. Once major filming began in 2000, Gilliam's worst fears were confirmed when a torrential storm washed away a major location and the actor playing the title character was too sick to perform. Production shut down immediately.

I WAS JUST MINDING MY OWN BUSINESS, WHEN . . .

When bad things

happen to good, bad,

and indifferent people

FLOOD ACTS AS DELIVERY SERVICE FOR ANGEL OF DEATH

2003: A man was gathering grass near a river in Assam Province, India, when a huge rhinoceros, which seemed to materialize out of thin air, charged and killed him. Monsoon floods had picked up the rhino at the Kaziranga National Park and deposited him downriver next to the unlucky man.

BUT IS IT ART? AVANT-GARDE MEMBER HELD BY POLICE

January 2000: Police officers in Manchester, New Hampshire, stopped a man who was walking down the street dressed as a giant penis. Drivers and pedestrians slowed down to stare at him. When officers asked him what he was doing and why, he replied, "It's art." Several passersby expressed their contempt for the penis-and-scrotum getup, and when the man refused to take it off, he was arrested for lewdness.

THE GREAT BOSTON MOLASSES FLOOD

January 15, 1919: On an unseasonably warm day, a giant vat at the Purity Distilling Company ruptured, spilling two million gallons of molasses onto the streets of Boston's North End. The ocean of syrup flowed through the streets, swallowing people and toppling buildings from their foundations. Hundreds of residents had to be cut from their clothing to free them from the sticky mess. People fleeing the area tracked molasses throughout the city, which smelled sweet for over a week.

BULLWINKLE DROPS IN AT LOCAL GREENHOUSE

2002: A 400-pound moose taking a leisurely stroll through downtown Anchorage, Alaska, stepped over a deck railing onto what it must have thought was a pristine snowy field, only to come crashing through the roof of a local greenhouse. Three of the unfortunate animal's legs punched through the fiberglass tiles, leaving it dangling eight feet above the ground for more than three hours. Rescuers tranquillized the moose and carefully pulled it out using a net and a backhoe. The animal then wandered off, dazed, his only injury a bruised ego.

COW CREAMS TURKISH COFFEE

2001: A Turkish man innocently playing dominoes in his local coffeehouse got the surprise of his life when a cow came crashing through the ceiling and landed on him. He woke up in the hospital hours later with a broken leg, many stitches, and a bevy of incredulous friends and relatives. The cow (uninjured) had wandered onto the roof of the café, which was built into the side of a hill.

SOMETIMES THE SKY REALLY IS FALLING . . .

IT'S RAINING—COWS!

2002: While speeding around the turns on a mountain road in Norway, a man spotted a large object falling ahead of him. He barely stopped his car before a huge cow hit the road right in front of him. The cow had been walking on a path high above the road and had somehow stumbled off the mountain. The driver later said, "To die under a suicide cow is probably the most idiotic death that can only be imagined." (No doubt something was lost in the translation.)

OCCUPATIONAL HAZARDS

Workplace perils

that OSHA never

thought of

CARPENTER GETS SCREWED

2003: A Truckee, California, construction worker who fell from a ladder onto a drill miraculously survived having his head impaled on an 18-inch drill bit. Although it destroyed his right eye, the metal bit completely missed his brain. Surgeons simply unscrewed the bit to get it out.

CHEF BITTEN BY DINNER AND DIES

2002: A poisonous reptile bit a Vietnamese chef who was retrieving it from its tank to kill it for use in an exotic porridge that called for snake's blood. He died on the way to the hospital.

Waste not, Want not: Another chef managed to fish the offending snake out of the aquarium safely and promptly served it to another customer.

SCREWDRIVERS FREE FISHERMAN FROM SHARK'S JAWS

2002: On a boat off the coast of Australia, a 20-year-old fisherman got his arms caught in a shark's jaws. The six-foot shark had been pulled up by accident in the fishermen's nets, and the young man was attempting to throw it back into the ocean when it grabbed him. Quick-thinking shipmates used screwdrivers to pry the unfortunate man from the clutches of the fish's maw and delivered him into the arms of the local hospital airlift.

WARNING

Sharks may be present

Shark bites have occurred in this area

LABORER SHOWS BOSS WHO'S CHEF

2002: A Nigerian farm laborer, who had a bitter argument with his boss about his pay, chopped her up with a machete and used her internal organs to make pepper soup. He confessed to the crime only after the soup made him vomit. Police also suspected a profit motive for the butchery—they think the man intended to sell the body parts to practitioners of witchcraft who believe that using human eyes, tongues, skulls, and genitals in their rituals can turn them into instant millionaires.

FLOYD COLLINS TRAPPED IN CRYSTAL CAVE

January 1925: Spelunker Floyd Collins's dream was to find a connection to the Mammoth Cave System in Kentucky through the caverns and tunnels on his own property. As he neared the exit of Crystal Cave after an unsuccessful search, a minor cave-in dropped a 27-pound rock on his leg, trapping him in a tight passage only 120 feet from the exit. Experts were unable to free him and feared that blasting would collapse the whole cave. Amputation was deemed too risky to Collins and any doctor willing to squeeze into the passage with him. A media circus congregated at the cave's entrance, and day-by-day accounts appeared in newspapers nationwide. Collins died of exposure after 15 days. The events inspired Billy Wilder's movie *Ace in the Hole* and a musical, *Floyd Collins*.

SEA BOSS FROM HELL, PART 1:

MUTINY ON THE HIGH SEAS

April 1789: After enduring the ranting and dictatorial rule of Captain William Bligh, the crew of the *Bounty,* led by second-in-command Fletcher Christian, mutinied. The captain and his few supporters were the lucky ones—set adrift in an open boat, they made it to safety and exoneration by the British court. The mutineers returned to Tahiti, took on a small cohort of native men and women, and, after searching for a place beyond the reach of the British Royal Navy, settled on Pitcairn's Island in the South Pacific. Dividing up the island was easy, but there were not enough women to go around, which led to years of infighting, rebellion, and killing. By the early 1800s, only one of the original mutineers was still alive—and he and his kin renounced uncharitable behavior for pious living.

SEA BOSS FROM HELL, PART 2:
MUTINY ON THE RIVER

English explorer Henry Hudson had a reputation for irascibility and foolhardiness— he discovered the

waterways that bear his name by accident and with a hostile crew in tow. In 1610, he set sail to find the fabled Northwest Passage and became ice-locked in what would become known as Hudson Bay for the winter. After barely surviving starvation, boredom, and other maladies, his crew mutinied in June 1611, when Hudson insisted they continue northwest rather than set sail for home. Hudson, his son, and seven others were set adrift in a small boat, never to be seen again. The mutineers returned to England and were never charged with any crime.

THINK BEFORE YOU SWALLOW

2003: Doctors in Irkutsk, Russia, in an effort to get people to be careful about putting things in their mouths, exhibited 3,000 items that had been surgically removed from patients' stomachs. The display ran the gamut from real and false teeth to needles, nails, fishhooks, glass, and metal objects that had been placed in the mouth during work and were inadvertently swallowed.

CARPENTER SURVIVES DUEL WITH NAIL GUN

2000: *The New England Journal of Medicine* published archive-worthy X-rays of "the luckiest guy in the world," according to the radiology professor who performed the X-ray. The man, a carpenter, walked into a hospital with his lower eyelid tacked down by a three-inch steel nail that had penetrated his head. The nail, shot into a board by a coworker, broke the wood and landed in the patient's face but managed to miss his tear duct, as well as a dozen vital organs, arteries, and nerves.

ALLIGATOR WRESTLER BURIES HEAD IN WORK

1998: An alligator wrestler in Florida, seeking to spice up his act, thrust his head into the reptile's mighty jaws. The gator, apparently stimulated by drops of sweat rolling off his partner's face, clamped down for several remorseless minutes until his jaws were pried open with metal pipes. After being treated at the hospital for face and head wounds, the wrestler planned to return to work.

THE SHOCK OF YOUR LIFE

Man meets electricity,

without the benefit

of insulation.

MISPLACED LEAK PROVES FATAL

2003: When a man in Bangkok, Thailand, stopped to relieve himself next to an electrical pole, he literally got the life shocked out of him. The dead man was wearing a prosthetic leg, which city technicians think might have been a strong electrical conductor, especially if there was even a slight power leak from the pole.

DAD GIVES DAUGHTER'S BEAU A SHOCKING WELCOME

2003: The stepfather of a 21-year-old woman in Germany made a very strong impression on her new boyfriend by allegedly giving him a shock with a cattle prod. The boyfriend hoped to make an impression of his own when the man appeared in court on assault charges.

ZEPPELIN ZAPPED BY ELECTRICAL STORM

September 3, 1925: The U.S. Navy dirigible USS *Shenandoah* catapulted to fame after a record-setting round-trip cross-country flight, but it met its end less than a year later during an electrical storm over Marietta, Ohio. High winds ripped the ship apart—14 of the 21 crewmembers were killed.

Adding income to injury: The owner of the farm on which the wreck landed charged $1.00 per car and $0.25 per pedestrian to see the ruin.

LIGHTNING STRIKES THE SAME PLACE TWICE . . . AND THEN SOME

The "Human Lightning Rod," Roy Sullivan (1912–1983), holds the world record for surviving the greatest number of lightning strikes. A United States forest ranger in the Shenandoah National Park in Virginia, he was struck on seven separate occasions while out in the field, including two strikes in the head (in 1972 and 1973) that set his hair on fire.

What Happens when the Lights Go Out in the "City That Never Sleeps"?

- **November 9, 1965:** Power went out at the height of rush hour, stranding more than 800,000 people in New York City and affecting 30 million more throughout the region. A relay in a Niagara generating station had failed, blacking out most of the northeastern United States and parts of Canada. Electricity was restored 13 hours later.

- **July 13-14, 1977:** Lightning struck New York metropolitan-area power plants, cutting off power to more than 10 million city residents for more than 24 hours. In contrast to 1965, the 1977 blackout was a billion-dollar disaster for the city. Rioting and looting engulfed entire neighborhoods. Fire department officials logged more than 1,000 fires, and almost 4,000 people were arrested.

- **August 14-15, 2003:** The largest blackout in American history began when unusually high electrical demand caused a power plant in Ohio to go off-line, creating a cascading failure in generators across the northeast electrical grid. At least 50 million people in the United States and Canada were without power for as long as two days. Although there was looting in Brooklyn, New York's latest blackout was, for the most part, quiet compared to the chaos of 1977.

HEINOUS HOLIDAYS TO YOU

The approach of Christmas brings harassment and dread to many excellent people. They have to buy a cartload of presents, and they never know what to buy to hit the various tastes; they put in three weeks of hard and anxious work, and when Christmas morning comes they are so dissatisfied with the result and so disappointed that they want to sit down and cry. Then they give thanks that Christmas comes but once a year.

—Mark Twain

PARENTS MAKE SANTA'S LIFE A LIVING HELL

2000: Parents in Germany were pressing Santa to dole out severe warnings to their kids—regarding homework, room cleaning, and sibling rivalry—instead of Christmas cheer. Many department-store Santas were disgusted by the requests; the job of reprimanding children has always fallen to Krampus, the German anti-Santa who punishes bad children at Christmastime.

OFFICIALS, FEARING FEROCIOUS PARENTS, CANCEL EGG HUNT

1992: Sh*tty parents sometimes happen to children, which was the case when officials of the St. Louis, Missouri, annual Easter egg hunt said enough is enough and called off the event. For four years, officials had been observing parents' mounting aggression, which culminated at the 1991 celebration, at which parents broke through police ribbons early and knocked aside hapless Boy Scout volunteers and wee children to get at the 20,000 hidden eggs.

CHRISTMAS CURMUDGEON TERRORIZES TOTS

There is no santa!

2002: A class of five-year-olds in Coral Springs, Florida, didn't know what hit them when a substitute teacher told them there was no Santa Claus. Parents demanded disciplinary action, but school officials said the teacher hadn't violated Board of Ed rules. Instead, they sent a "Santa" with a real white beard to the classroom to mollify the children and their irate parents.

ENGLISH CHAINSAW MASSACRE?

2002: A man in Lincolnshire, England, thought the grim reaper had finally come for him when someone showed up at his house brandishing a huge, roaring chainsaw. Luckily, the chainsaw-toting man was heading for a Halloween costume party in the neighborhood and had gone to the wrong address.

BULLWINKLE SPOOKED BY ROCKY HORROR SHOW IN SNOW

2001: When two kids decked out for trick or treating ran across their front yard in Anchorage, Alaska, they startled a moose that had been resting on the ground near some trees. The bull moose charged the kids, knocked them down, and fled. A local biologist said that Halloween is a traumatic time for these animals, which are unaccustomed to encountering costumed kids running all over the place.

Puritanism. The haunting fear that someone, somewhere, may be happy.

—H. L. MENCKEN

PURITANS ABOLISH CHRISTMAS: DON'T EAT, DON'T DRINK, BE MISERABLE

1644: Rioting broke out regularly all over England during the reign of Oliver Cromwell, beginning in 1644, when the Puritan parliament outlawed Christmas and replaced it with a day of fasting to repent for making the holiday into a time of "giving liberty to carnall [sic] and sensual delights." The laws were unenforceable, the rioting unstoppable, and Christmas was finally restored, along with the monarchy, in 1660.

EASTER BUNNY SHOULD HAVE KEPT GOING . . . AND GOING

2000: Unwilling to traumatize the children, police in Wisconsin waited until the Easter bunny in the Janesville Mall was done with photos and greetings before  arresting him for shoplifting. Days before, security guards lost a man who allegedly swiped a pair of sneakers but later recognized him on the security video as the mall's Easter bunny.

Silver lining: As far as the mall manager knows, Santa Claus has a clean record.

DISTURBING THE PEACE ON EARTH

2000: A group of Cistercian monks living on Caldy Island, off the coast of Wales, had anything but a silent night when a guest staying at the monastery for Christmas got drunk and started a midnight serenade of Christmas carols. The monks, who observe a vow of silence and do not speak for 12 hours every night, were unable to tell him to shut up. "All we could do was lie in our beds and cover our ears," one monk said. The man, who had been visiting the monks for over 30 years, was still welcome, provided he left his booze on the mainland.

HOLIDAY DECORATIONS SEND MAN OVER EDGE

2001: A Washington man, enraged by several mishaps with Christmas decorations, got thrown in jail when he took it out on his own backyard.

The trouble began when he discovered that the Christmas lights had been carelessly balled up at the end of the previous season. He was patiently untangling the long string of lights and laying it out in his driveway when his daughter, unaware of the project, barreled home and ran over all the lights. Thankfully, instead of killing his family or himself, the man took his gun and shot up his empty backyard. Five officers showed up to arrest him.

INSANE SANTAS VANDALIZE SAN FRANCISCO

December 1995: Dozens of disorderly Santas rampaged through San Francisco's downtown commercial district, ripping up and stealing Christmas decorations, harassing holiday shoppers, and crashing a children's carnival. Three were arrested, one for indecent exposure.

The event was organized by the San Francisco Cacophony Society, which later apologized for any harm done.

WAITING FOR DOOMSDAY

Sh*t that was

supposed to

happen but—in

most cases—didn't.

ALL GOOD THINGS MUST COME TO AN END . . .

The Paleocene Epoch: Sixty-five million years ago a comet or asteroid as big as Mount Everest slammed into Earth near the Yucatán Peninsula. It produced continent-wide fires, earthquakes, 100-foot tsunamis, and a debris cloud that darkened the skies worldwide for years. Countless millions died. Hundreds of species, including the dinosaurs, went extinct.

Silver lining: The eradication of *T. rex* and his cronies allowed the rise of mammals; big bucks for museum directors, toy manufacturers, Michael Crichton, and Steven Spielberg (all mammals).

NOAH-BRAINER . . .

The 16th Century: In the 16th century, men of reason used science to warn their fellow citizens of imminent disaster—often with unpredictable results:

Count von Iggleheim wasn't taking any chances. In 1499, German astrologer

and mathematician Johannes Stöffler predicted that "the world will end by a giant flood on February 20, 1524," so Iggleheim built a three-story ark just in case. The flood never came, but disaster did—when it rained on February 20, the local mob panicked and stampeded the ark, crushing Iggleheim to death.

CHRISTMAS COMET PORTENDS GREAT PLAGUE

The 17th Century: Black plague had already broken out on the Continent by 1663, and the anxious British feared the worst when a comet suddenly appeared in the skies over London during Christmas of 1664. It was instantly seen as a portent of doom. The doom that did, in fact, immediately follow was two months of ice storms, which temporarily cut off trade between Britain and continental Europe.

A second comet appeared in March 1665, causing a renewal of fears, which, unfortunately, were duly fulfilled. April's thaw brought plague across the Channel and killed tens of thousands before the Great Fire of London, in September of the following year, purged the city of disease.

FOR WHOM THE BELL TOLLS . . .

The 18th Century: Basing his predictions on earthquakes that had taken place four weeks apart on February and March 8, 1761, William Bell predicted that London would be destroyed on April 5, 28 days after the preceding quake, sending people into a panic. When nothing happened, Bell faced neither assault nor arrest—after all, this was the Age of Enlightenment. Instead, he was summarily tossed into Bedlam, London's infamous insane asylum.

IT'S MILLER TIME . . .

The 19th Century: By the 19th century, authorities had bigger fish to fry than local prophets of doom. They let William Miller's followers vote with their feet:

In the 1840s, William Miller published a book predicting that the end of the world would come between March 21, 1843, and March 21, 1844. More than 100,000 "Millerites" were drawn to his flock and patiently waited out the end. When it didn't come as predicted, one of the faithful began recalculating the date of doom to October 22. When nothing happened then, either, Miller's ministry disbanded, and he disappeared from public life.

SECOND (COMING) NOTICE . . .

The 20th Century: By the 20th century, law enforcement was not needed to keep most doomsayers in line—the forces of market capitalism were strong enough to do the job:

In September 1975, an Arkansas woman convinced 21 members of her family that the end was near. To await the second coming, they took up residence in her house until the following July, when marshals came and threw them all out of the house. Figuring doomsday was just around the corner, the woman had neglected to pay her mortgage, and the bank had foreclosed on her house.

THE MILLENIUM BUG WITH NO BITE . . .

The Year 2000: Cory Hamasaki, Y2K consultant, November 1998: "We must prepare ourselves for the very real possibility that the outcome of this situation might be the total extinction of the entire human race. It really could be worse than I am predicting, and I really am being optimistic. First, I would like to assure you that I am not some kind of nut anxiously waiting for the end of the world . . ."

NOT WITH A BANG BUT A WHIMPER . . .

In 1997, astronomers identified a large asteroid that they predicted would pass very close to Earth, with a small chance of impact, on October 26, 2028. Doomsday scenarists had a field day, predicting an end to humankind much like what had befallen the dinosaurs. A few years later, astronomers revised their figures and said the rock would not get any nearer to Earth than more than twice the distance from the earth to the moon.

SH*T HAPPENS

Sometimes when

we say "sh*t

happens," we mean

it literally . . .

PILE OF EXCREMENT BUILT TO SAVE HUMAN RACE

1973: A concerned and caring California man began building a "living monument" in his backyard to save mankind from calamity. By 1990, the monument, now a 30-foot-tall work made of horse and cow dung, had become a nose- and eyesore to all who lived near it. On the other hand, the plague-size swarm of flies it attracted were delighted.

SOMETIMES THE SKY REALLY IS FALLING . . .

IT'S RAINING— SEWAGE!

1992: Like an innocent child catching snowflakes on his tongue during the first snowfall of the season, a Kentucky farmer took a lick of a greenish icicle that fell from the sky only to discover it was frozen human waste inadvertently released from a passing airplane.

Falling frozen sewage is not uncommon. In 1992 baseball-size chunks of green ice crashed through the roof into the living room of a house in Washington state, where the family was watching a football game. The owner philosophized, "It's a good thing none of us was killed. . . . What would you put on the tombstone?"

CHRISTMAS THIEF GETS POOPED OUT

2002: A thief at the Stonebriar Centre mall outside Dallas, Texas, thought he was getting away with a big haul when he swiped two huge plastic bags from the back of a truck parked outside the mall. "Oh, sh*t!" he exclaimed on inspecting the bags' contents. The truck belonged to the owner of an animal-waste disposal company.

JURY SUMMONS SEES PLACE SUN DOESN'T SHINE

2002: A jury-duty summons is rarely received with joy, but a Westport, Connecticut, man's brutally honest response got him a trial of his own. After scribbling the words "Stop wasting paper" on the summons, the man followed his own advice and used it to wipe himself before returning the notice to the court clerk. Police later arrested him for harassment and breach of the peace.

Stop wasting paper

CUTTING SCAT OFF AT THE SOURCE

2002: Town councilors in Wiltshire, England, in a desperate effort to discourage pigeons from gathering, asked local supermarkets to stop selling stale bread to people who scatter it outside. The extremely well fed birds had been relieving themselves everywhere in great quantities, ruining flowerbeds, defacing monuments, and generally running down the quality of town life.

POLICE RUN IN RING-AND-RUN DUNG RING

2003: Two men in their 50s thought they'd had the last laugh when they dumped dozens of bags of dog poop in front of a house in Michigan in order to settle a score with the owner. Police caught them and wiped the smiles off their faces with big-ticket summonses for littering.

ELEPHANT DUMPS KEEPER

1998: A zookeeper was in the wrong place at the wrong time when an elephant unloaded more than 200 pounds of dung on him, smothering him under the mess. The elephant had been constipated, and the keeper had given him 22 doses of animal laxative, a bushel of berries and prunes, and was about to administer an olive oil enema when the elephant finally relieved itself.

MAN STRANDED IN FIRST CIRCLE OF HELL

2000: A 75-year-old Virginia man, who walked with the aide of a crutch, nonetheless insisted on using the outhouse he'd built for himself more than 50 years before on his rural homestead. When he made a pit stop one Saturday night, the floor caved in. The man was suspended over the pit by the broken oak floorboards but couldn't get out. His ordeal lasted until his mailman heard his cries 69 hours later. After his rescue, the man compared his experiences to being in "the Bible's hell," and he said the worst part was fighting off the rats, spiders, insects, and snakes that also frequented the place.

A final word

What to do once the ultimate sh*t has happened to you:

- Fulfill your dreams of brilliance. The folks at www.lifegem.com can turn your decomposing remains into a perfect, eternal one-carat diamond.

- "Beam Me Up, Scotty." Join James Doohan (the "real" Scotty), Gene Roddenberry (the creator of *Star Trek*), and hundreds of others in outer space. Contact Celestis, a private space-exploration company (http://memorialspaceflights.com), to learn how your ashes can literally get to heaven.

- Let future generations grow up under your watchful gaze: The historically minded staff at Summum (www.summum.org) will mummify your corpse and preserve it in an Egyptian-style casket, which even your distant descendants will be proud to display as part of their home décor.

- Help save the planet: Instead of eating up a room-size chunk of real estate with your family plot or mausoleum, get an ecofriendly biodegradable coffin at a cemetery like Forever Fernwood in Mill Valley, California, where you will literally become part of the landscape within months of your interment. As Thomas Lynch, an author and funeral director in Michigan said, "It is not enough to be a corpse anymore. Now, you have to be a politically correct corpse."

Photo Credits

page 8: The Granger Collection; **page 14:** Library of Congress; **page 20:** Mary Evans Picture Library; **page 22:** Library of Congress; **page 27:** Library of Congress; **page 29:** LEBRECHT MUSIC & ARTS; **page 41:** AP/Wide World Photos; **page 47:** Mary Evans Picture Library; **page 70:** Library of Congress; **page 88:** AP/Wide World Photos; **page 94:** Library of Congress; **page 97:** Library of Congress; **page 106:** Library of Congress; **page 107:** AP/Wide World Photos; **page 109:** Library of Congress; **page 113:** Mary Evans Picture Library; **page 116:** AP/Wide World Photos; **page 126:** Library of Congress; **page 129:** The Granger Collection, New York; **page 140:** AP/Wide World Photos; **page 146:** AP/Wide World Photos; **page 147:** Library of Congress; **page 148:** Mary Evans Picture Library; **page 149:** Mary Evans Picture Library; **page 166:** AP/Wide World Photos; **page 167:** Photofest; **page 171:** AP/Wide World Photos; **page 184:** AP/Wide World Photos; **page 189:** Mary Evans Picture Library; **page 196:** Mary Evans Picture Library; **page 199:** Library of Congress ; **page 203:** The Granger Collection, New York; **page 208:** The Granger Collection, New York; **page 211:** AP/Wide World Photos; **page 230:** Beauvais Cathedral, Beauvais, France/Peter Willi/ The Bridgeman Art Library ; **page 231:** AP/Wide World Photos; **page 233:** AP/Wide World Photos; **page 234:** AP/Wide World Photos; **page 245:** AP/Wide World Photos; **page 250:** AP/Wide World Photos; **page 266:** Everglades National Park; **page 287:** Photofest; **page 289:** Mary Evans Picture Library; **page 295:** AP/Wide World Photos; **page 309:** Mary Evans Picture Library; **page 312:** Mary Evans Picture Library; **page 314:** AP/Wide World Photos.

About The Author

Debbie Lazarus is a housewife from hell who lives in suburban New York with her family. She enjoys going to the movies, trolling through history books, and will do almost anything to avoid cooking dinner.